Total Quality Management

Springer
Berlin
Heidelberg
New York
Barcelona
Hong Kong
London
Milan
Paris
Singapore
Tokyo

Hubert K. Rampersad

Total Quality Management

An Executive Guide
to Continuous Improvement

With 62 Figures and 42 Tables

 Springer

Professor Dr. Ir. Hubert Rampersad
E-mail: hubert_rampersad@hotmail.com

ISBN 3-540-67967-7 Springer-Verlag Berlin Heidelberg New York

Cataloging-in-Publication Data applied for
Die Deutsche Bibliothek - CIP-Einheitsaufnahme
Rampersad, Hubert K.: Total quality management: an executive guide to continuous improvement / Hubert K. Rampersad. – Berlin; Heidelberg; New York; Barcelona; Hong Kong; London; Milan; Paris; Singapore; Tokyo: Springer, 2001
  ISBN 3-540-67967-7

Springer-Verlag Berlin Heidelberg New York
a member of BertelsmannSpringer Science+Business Media GmbH

© Springer-Verlag Berlin · Heidelberg 2001
Printed in Germany

Hardcover-Design: Erich Kirchner, Heidelberg

SPIN 10733710   42/2202-5 4 3 2 1 0 - Printed on acid-free paper

*This book is dedicated
to my wife Rita and my sons Rodney and Warren*

Preface

Total Quality Management (TQM) is both a philosophy and a set of guidelines that form the basis for continuous and gradual quality improvement of the total organization, whereby planning of improvement activities, implementation of these plans, checking and undertaking actions, is continuously taking place. This philosophy includes a common method to improve the entire organization in a step by step, structured and systematic manner, and is also based on a consistent application of available quality improvement tools and techniques. The TQM-concept is related to the continuous and gradual improvement of all employees at all levels within the organization, in order to improve their personal output on a daily basis. It provides a framework within which you may continuously and routinely improve everything you do in order to better meet internal and external customer needs, and to continuously increase shareholder value. TQM is a journey toward improvement and this book will guide you on that never-ending journey. By making continuous improvement a part of your daily routine, you will integrate it into all aspects of your work. This should become your organization's way of life.

This book is meant to help you with the continuous improvement of your daily workload, in order to reach a high quality product, controllable costs, and loyal customers. This benefits the competitive position of your organization and creates the opportunity for you to grow and excel. For this purpose, it is imperative that lessons are learned from the mistakes made, that a holistic and unambiguous approach is used to solve problems in a systematic and structured manner, and that your behavior is focused on realizing total quality. This book will assist you in the effective use of the available problem solving tools, and will aid you in applying the quality improvement process in all aspects of your work, based on a visionary approach. By systematically and routinely working according to the Total Quality Management philosophy in everything you do within your organization, you will be able to add increased value for internal and external customers and continually delight them. I think you will find this book indispensable in the new world of e-business and e-commerce.

This book is a synergistic product of minds and efforts of many thinkers, from which I have benefited. I am grateful for their inspiration. I am also grateful to Mauro Tuur and Trevie Feurich who played important roles in the preparation of this book. Thoughtful comments from Dennis Hays, former U.S. Ambassador to Suriname, and John Murphy of the Canada Customs Revenue Agency enabled me to make important improvements in the final manuscript.

I wish you a lot of success on the never-ending journey toward Total Quality Management.

January 2001   Hubert K. Rampersad

Contents

1 Introduction

Organizations can only survive by continuous quality improvement. An increasing number of organizations are beginning to perceive this and are continuously focussing on quality improvement, improvement of customer orientation, and reduction of costs and throughput times. After all, standing idle means moving backwards. Slogans of management gurus related to this concept such as: *do everything right the first time, improve continuously, restrict yourself to your core competencies, limit excess waste, deliver precisely on time, develop a learning organization and bring about a cultural change*, are finding their way more and more into most organizations. For this purpose, various concepts and philosophies are used such as: *Total Quality Management, Kaizen, Benchmarking, Business Process Re-engineering, Lean Production, and Just in Time.*

The Total Quality Management concept, in which the Kaizen philosophy is imbedded, is the central point in this book. This Japanese concept forms the basis for ongoing quality improvement of the entire organization. Quality encompasses the continuous fulfillment of the customer's expectations at the agreed upon conditions. TQM, which aims at continuous quality improvement at all levels of the organization is used to achieve this goal. Experience shows that continuous attention for TQM results in a qualitatively better product and service, a more customer-focused organization culture, reduced variability in processes, improved customer satisfaction, and improved competitive advantage. It benefits customers, the organization and its members, and society in general.

This book will guide you on the never-ending journey toward continuous and routine improvement of yourself, your work and your organization. For this purpose, the "what" and "why" of TQM will first be discussed in chapter 2. In the following chapters 3 to 5, light will be shed on the elements of TQM by means of practical examples. In this way, the problem solving discipline and the accompanying tools and techniques will be discussed in chapter 3. In chapter 4, the interpersonal skills are stated whereby the communication process and communicative skills are discussed in depth. Teamwork is central in chapter 5, with more discussion on building team performance, and the role of both the team members and the team leader. The quality improvement process is discussed in chapter 6. It concerns a method for working systematically, disciplined, and as a team to accomplish continuous quality improvement of the entire organization. Many firms fail to get positive results from TQM because of the way in which it is implemented. Successful implementation of TQM requires a multi disciplinary and project-matic approach, and the realization of a cultural change. The organization of the implementation process is central in chapter 7. The cultural aspects are discussed in chapter 8, with topics such as how to realize a cultural change and how to deal with resistance against organizational changes. An integral step by step plan is presented in chapter 9 to accomplish continuous improvement and effective implementation of the TQM-concept within the organization on the basis of an inspiring personal and organizational mission and vision. Finally chapter 10 focuses on some concluding comments.

Learning objectives

While reading and after studying this book:

➤ You will be able to better adapt your working method to the realization of total quality.

➤ You will be acquainted with the tools and techniques in the context of the problem solving discipline and with their application within your organization.

➤ You will learn how to develop interpersonal skills and how to apply these in all areas of your work.

➤ You will learn how to successfully generate innovative ideas.

➤ You will learn how to effectively work as a team and how to coach teams successfully.

➤ You will learn how to become an effective and a visionary leader.

➤ You will learn how to create a work climate in which people are happy, productive, and continuously learning from mistakes.

➤ You will learn how to execute quality improvement processes in a multidisciplinary and structured manner in order to solve organizational problems in a holistic way.

➤ You will learn how to continuously control the quality of your products and services.

➤ You will learn how to reduce your quality costs.

➤ You will learn how to improve your customer orientation.

➤ You will learn how to integratively deal with quality projects based on an inspiring personal and organizational mission, vision, related core values, and SMART goals.

➤ You will learn how to deal with resistance against organizational changes and how to realize a cultural change in your organization.

➤ You will learn how to successfully organize the implementation of TQM, based on a visionary approach.

➤ You will be able to maximize the opportunities of e-business and e-commerce.

➤ You will be able to continuously increase shareholder value.

2 Total Quality Management

Total quality management is both a philosophy and a set of guiding principles that represent the foundation of a continuously improving organization. It encompasses mobilizing the entire organization to satisfy the demands of the customers. TQM is focused on routine involvement and participation of everyone in the organization in the systematic improvement of quality. It involves each individual and group within all parts of the organization. TQM provides a way of life to constantly improve the performance at every level and in every activity, by creating a positive continuous improvement environment based on teamwork, trust and respect, examining the process through which work gets done in a systematic, consistent, organizationwide manner, applying quantitative methods and analytical techniques, and expanding your knowledge and expertise in process improvement. According to Deming's chain reaction, this allows a firm to capture a larger market share and provide more job security (see figure 2.1).

Figure 2.1 Deming's Chain Reaction

> *To me, quality is a state of mind... The relentless pursuit of excellence, of never being satisfied with what you do, how you do it and how quickly you do it. There is always room for improvement. Everything can always be done better. Quality should be part of our soul.*
>
> Jan D. Timmer, former President of Philips Electronics

TQM is a continuous learning pocess which never stops. It is a cyclic, iterative, and never-ending activity (Crosby, 1984). It can be seen as a logical extension of the way quality has progressed (see figure 2.2). The use of standard quality systems such as ISO 9001-9003 norms make up the first steps on the way to total quality, as is illustrated in figure 2.3

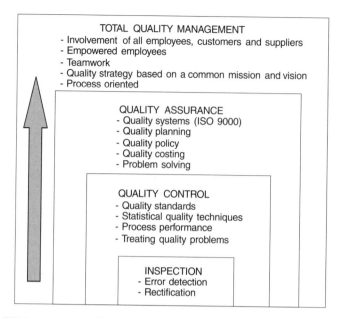

Figure 2.2 TQM represents a shift from traditional approaches to quality

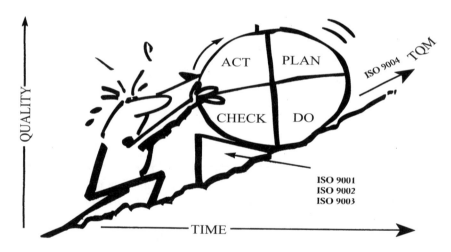

Figure 2.3 Continuous improvement toward TQM

TQM is a disciplined method of defining a problem, observing it, determining its root causes, taking action, checking the effectiveness of that action, standardizing the solution, and evaluating the process. It could be seen as being concerned with the following (Slack, et al., 1995):

- meeting the needs and expectations of customers;
- covering all parts of the organization;
- examining all costs which are related to quality;
- *doing things right the first time,* i.e. quality designing rather than inspecting;
- developing the systems and procedures which support quality and improvement;
- developing a continuous process of improvement.

Therefore, this approach works equally well in manufacturing firms and in sevice organizations. TQM concerns incremental and ongoing improvement of yourself, your work, and your entire organization. This is known as *Kaizen* in Japanese (Imai, 1985). The Kaizen philosophy is imbedded in the TQM-concept and encompasses the continuous and gradual improvement of all employees in the organization, in order to improve their personal output on a daily basis. Some important Kaizen rules are:

- work with and according to a guideline;
- problems are opportunities for improvement;
- retrieve information there where it happens;
- consider the facts;
- work according to a plan;
- avoid waste;
- order and neatness;
- keep appointments.

In the Kaizen approach, the *"Deming-wheel"* is central, existing of a cycle of activities necessary for effective quality improvement, see figure 2.2 (Deming, 1985). This cycle consists of the following four phases: Plan, Do, Check, and Act.

Plan: Define the problem, analyze the causes and draft an action plan for solving the problem, determine the quality objectives and the critical success factors, define the performance indicators, collect and analyze the necessary process data, generate possible solutions, select the most feasible solution, and work it out.

Do: First, implement the plan on a limited scale or conduct an experiment to test the proposed improvement. Collecting data is hereby essential. Train all involved employees in the use of quality improvement methods and techniques. Describe the process which is considered for improvement and form project teams to lead the process.

Check: Evaluate the trial project with the performance indicators. Verify whether the improvement has been successful. What have we learned?

Act: Act to implement proven improvements. The choices are: introduce the plan, adjust or reject it. The improvements are documented in standard procedures so all employees involved are well-informed on how to handle in future. Usually, the cycle will be repeated under the different circumstances and conditions to test how consistent the results are.

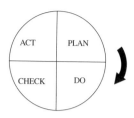

Figure 2.4 De PDCA-cycle

By continuously following the PDCA-cycle and accepting that this cycle never stops, improvement will become part of every person's job. The organization will learn to understand itself better and is therefore better equipped to deal with the wishes of the customer.

The TQM-concept is based on a number of quality principles, which are illustrated in table 2.1.

Table 2.1: Quality principles

Customer focus and customer involvement	**Consistency of purpose**
– Employees regularly visit their customers. – Customers are known and understood. – Customers' needs are integrated in the activities. – More is being done than the customer expects. – Satisfied customers are priority number one. – Changing customers needs are systematically collected and lead to improvement. – Preventing complaints instead of reacting to complaints.	– An inspiring mission and vision is developed and communicated to all organizational levels. – SMART-goals are formulated and preserved *(Specific, Measurable, Achievable, Realistic, and Time specific).* – Managers are consistent in their behavior regarding these goals. – Guidance is given to the quality improvement process. – There is commitment at top management.
Involvement of all employees	**Act according to facts**
– Voluntary total involvement of everyone. – Teamwork that leverage the knowledge and provides synergy, based on open-communication, respect and trust. – Skills are developed on the basis of *"Learning by doing".* – Decisions on the basis of consensus. – The present situation is open for discussion. – Investing in knowledge. – Empowered employees. – Entrepreneurial approach and leadership skills at all business levels.	– Work according to facts and not based on rumors or feelings. – The causes and consequences of problems are analyzed according to "measuring is knowing". – Goal oriented data is gathered and interpreted accordingly. – Measurements are based on figures; verify everything with data. – Quality costs are analyzed.

Table 2.1: (Continued)

Process oriented	Focus on continuous improvement
– Internal customers are also satisfied. – The process is more important than the results; address the means of work accomplishment an not only the outcomes. – The effectiveness of the process is measured. – The output is standardized. – The processes are documented in schemes and standard working procedures. – Suppliers are regarded as partners and long term relationships are established. – The TQM culture is expanded to suppliers. – Reduction of process variation occurs continuously.	– Employees improve themselves and their work and help others improve themselves and the organization. – Problems are regarded as a means for improvement and a chance to improve processes. – Emphasis on problem prevention instead of correction. – Improvements are based on a cross-functional, structured, and holistic approach, and are continuously documented. – Multidisciplinary improvement teams are established. – There is a working climate in which continuous improvement is a way of life. – Improvement of the whole and not just the parts.

These quality principles are related to Deming's and Crosby's 14 points for quality improvement (see table 2.2)

Table 2.2: Deming's and crosby's 14 points for quality improvement

No.	Deming	Crosby
1	Create constancy of purpose towards improvement of product and service	Establish management commitment
2	Adopt the new philosophy	Form interdepartmental quality improvement teams
3	Cease dependence on inspection	Establish quality measurement
4	End awarding business on the basis of price tag	Evaluate the cost of quality
5	Improve constantly the system of production and service	Establish quality awareness
6	Institute training on the job	Instigate corrective action
7	Institute leadership	Ad hoc committee for the zero defects programme
8	Drive out fear, so that everyone may work effectively for the company	Supervise employee training
9	Break down barriers between departments	Hold a zero defects day to let all employees realize that there has been a change
10	Eliminate slogans and exhortations	Encourage individuals to establish improvement goals for themselves and their groups

Table 2.2 (Continued)

11	Eliminate quotas or work standards	Error cause removal
12	Give people pride in their job	Recognize and appreciate those who participate
13	Institute education and a self-improvement programme	Establish quality councils to communicate on a regular basis
14	Put erveryone to work to accomplish it	Do it over again to emphasize that the quality improvement program never ends

There is only one valid definition of a business purpose: to create a satisfied customer. It is the customer who determines what the business is.

Peter Drucker

Total quality management is a common method to improve the whole organization stepwise, structured and systematically according to hard work, discipline, intensive training, and consistent implementation of techniques and resources. These quality principles form the foundation of TQM and are expressed in the four pillars of the TQM-house, see figure 2.5 (PA Consulting Group, 1991; Rampersad, 2000):

1. Problem Solving Discipline;
2. Interpersonal skills;
3. Teamwork;
4. Quality Improvement Process.

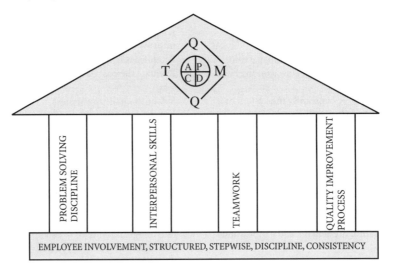

Figure 2.5 The four pillars of the TQM-house

The success of TQM improves proportionally in conjunction with the percentage of employees within the organization who master this quality attitude, mentality, and skills. The four elements of this concept will subsequently be described in separate chapters.

> *TQM covers all parts of the organization... For an organization to be truly effective, every single part of it, each department, each activity, each person and each level must work properly together, because every person and every activity affects and in turn is affected by others.*
>
> A. Muhlemann & J. Oakland

3 The Problem Solving Discipline

The Problem Solving Discipline (PSD) encompasses a methodology for systematic, gradual, and team wise solving of problems. It involves the first pillar of the TQM-house (see figure 3.1). The PSD comprises of six steps for adequate and team wise solving of problems, e.g. (Rampersad, 1994, and PA Consulting Group, 1991).

1. Defining the problem
2. Analyzing the causes
3. Generating solutions
4. Planning and implementing the solution
5. Measuring to determine if the solution really works
6. Standardization of the improvements

This process should be an important part of everybody's job. Figure 3.2 illustrates the six steps of the PSD. The methods and techniques used for each step will be discussed in paragraph 3.2.

> *Solving a problem may be easier than you think. You need a systematic approach.*
>
> W. Edwards Deming

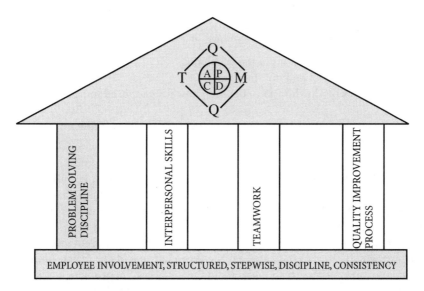

Figure 3.1 The first pillar of the TQM-house

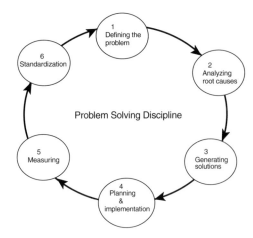

Figure 3.2 The Problem Solving Discipline

3.1 The PSD-approach

3.1.1 Step 1: Defining the problem

First of all, it is necessary to appoint an improvement team and define the problem through teamwork. A precise definition of the problem is essential to find the exact cause by which an effective solution can be generated (figure 3.3). For a clear description of the problem, the team needs to know which problems should be solved, where the problems occur and which aspects play a role. Therefore, it is necessary to consult several information sources on the subject, such as results of customer surveys, complaints of customers, information on process performance, and meeting with customers. A good formulation of a problem:

- defines the characteristics of the problem;
- identifies the effect and not the cause;
- concentrates on the difference between how it's supposed to be and how it is now;
- consists of an overall measurement of the problem; how frequent? how much? when?

It is also important for an accurate definition of the problem to know how the process is presently being conducted. Therefore, it is necessary to visualize the process with flow charts, whereby all stages from input to output are illustrated. The team should therefore also consult with employees directly involved in the process. It is also important to know whether the measures taken resulted in an improvement. This will require taking measurements at different points in the process, which are also indicated on the flow chart e.g. daily registration of the complaints. It is necessary to understand the details of the problem and translate the customer's needs into measurable and concrete specifications. Brainstorm

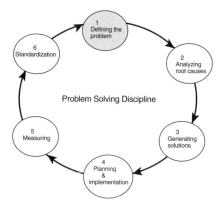

Figure 3.3 Defining the problem

widely about the problem. The following six words guarantee that all relevant questions about the problem are asked: *when? how? where? what? who? why? So: When does a problem occur? How do we know whether it occurs? How did the problem start? How urgent is the problem? Where does it occur? What is the problem? What are the causes? What are the consequences? Where are the limitations? Who causes it? Whose problem is it? Why does it occur?*

3.1.2 Step 2: Analyzing the root causes

This step aims at charting the many possible causes of the problem and selecting the most logical root cause from this (see figure 3.4). Make sure there is a systematic gathering of data at all key points in the process. Through brainstorming, take as many potential causes into consideration. A rule of thumb is to ask the question

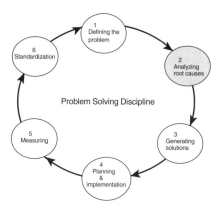

Figure 3.4 Analyzing the root causes

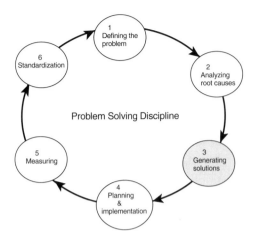

Figure 3.5 Generating solutions

"*Why?*" five times. Then, select the most logical causes for further analyses. In this instance, it concerns gathering and analysis of data through illustrative techniques such as graphs, Pareto-diagrams, and histograms to identify ongoing trends and the use of scatter diagrams to illustrate relationships (see § 3.2).

3.1.3 Step 3: Generating solutions

This step aims at generating possible solutions to solve the root cause of the problem, resulting in greater customer satisfaction (see figure 3.5). Brainstorm using the data from the previous steps and generate an extensive list of possible solutions. Evaluate the solutions and then choose the one with the best chance of success and which is most suited to solve the problem.

3.1.4 Step 4: Planning and implementation

This step aims at carefully planning the proposed improvements, considering the consequences, and then implementing the solution (figure 3.6). Therefore, it is important to communicate with all stakeholders regarding the proposed solution, make all plans clear, design procedures, identify potential barriers to implementation, consider all necessary resources (material, equipment, facilities, people), and identify training requirements.

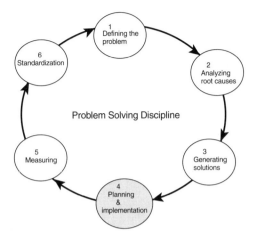

Figure 3.6 Planning and implementation

3.1.5 Step 5: Measuring

Measurements are completed to see whether the implemented solution has solved the problem or whether the problem has been reduced (see figure 3.7). A determination is also made to see whether the requirements of the customers are met. In case the requirements of the customers are still not being met, the possibility exists that the solution was incorrect, the problem was incorrectly defined and/or the wrong cause was treated. To measure the effectiveness of the implemented solution, several techniques and methods can be used (see § 3.2).

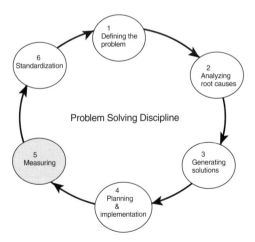

Figure 3.7 Measuring

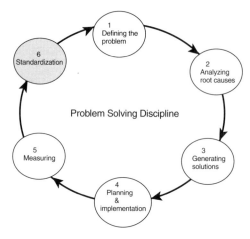

Figure 3.8 Standardization

3.1.6 Standardization

Standardization encompasses the clear establishment or documentation of process executions in standard procedures, and making sure that all employees involved in the process understand these and use them in a consistent manner. The purpose of this step is to incorporate the new process into the daily routine (see figure 3.8). This will also prevent the organization from returning to old habits. One should take the following aspects into consideration:

- make sure that the procedures become part of the daily routine;
- make sure that all procedures are known and understood by everyone;
- give the information gathered during evaluation to those responsible for the process;
- each modification to the process has to be documented in changed procedures;
- communicate as much as possible with employees regarding the measures taken and the results achieved;
- allow the process operators to document the procedures.

Before the improvement team is dissolved, the functioning of the team has to be evaluated by the team members to learn from their experiences. Then, the team should consider whether the solution could be implemented in other sectors within the organization.

3.2 Most important tools and techniques

To execute the problem solving discipline successfully, it is necessary to apply certain quality improvement tools and techniques. A great number of appropriate tools and techniques are available for your continuous improvement effort. The most important among these are:

1. Brainstorming
2. Affinity diagram
3. Benchmarking
4. Fishbone diagram
5. Check sheet
6. Flow chart
7. Line graph
8. Run chart
9. Histogram
10. Pareto-diagram
11. Failure Mode and Effect Analysis
12. Scatter diagram
13. Control chart
14. Quality Function Deployment
15. Tree diagram

These tools and techniques are essential for the clear establishment of quality improvements. They are described according to the following parts: *What is it? When do you use it? How do you use it? and Example(s).* Some of these examples are derived from the recommended TQM-manual of PA Consulting Group (1991) and NEN-ISO 9004-4 (1993).

3.2.1 Brainstorming

What is it?

Brainstorming encompasses the systematic and structured generation of possible ideas, on the basis of the creative thinking of a group of people.

Four game rules:

1. Criticism is prohibited.
The participants of a brainstorming session should try not to think of usefulness, importance, feasibility and relevance, and may certainly not comment on these. Therefore, the review of ideas has to be postponed. This rule must not only lead to many but also to unexpected associations. Strictly adhearing to this rule is also essential to prevent team members from feeling attacked.

2. Generate ideas freely.
The purpose is for team members to express each idea. Each idea that surfaces has to be shared without fear for criticism. Therefore, in a brainstorming session, an

environment has to be created that gives team members a feeling of confidence and freedom.

3. Build upon ideas of others.
The team members have to generate ideas by building on ideas of others. One should look for combinations and improvements of ideas.

4. Try to generate as many ideas as possible.
In this case, quantity is more important than quality. The more ideas, the greater the chance of good solutions. The idea behind this is that quantity leads to quality.

When do you use it?

This technique can be used in all phases of the problem solving discipline to obtain a good idea of problems, causes, results, and solutions. The goal of brainstorming is to generate as many ideas as it takes to solve a problem.

How do you use it?

Steps in the brainstorming process:

Preparation:

1. Formulate the problem accurately. Complex problems should be divided into sub-problems if needed.
2. Form a group of five to eight members. Experts from various disciplines with the same status within the organization.
3. Select a team leader who coaches, steers, helps, and guides.
4. Send a note to the team members with the formulation of the problem and some background information some time before the session.
5. Organize a preparatory meeting with the team members immediately before the brainstorming session, in which the procedure and the game rules are explained. The problem is defined once again with the participants if necessary.

The formulation of the problem has to be clear to everyone, just like the delimitation of the problem. Defining the problem will often take longer than the brainstorming session itself, and should end in a formulation of the problem in the form of a question, such as: *How can we improve the efficiency of the purchase process? How can we shorten the throughput time of the production process?*

Execution of the brainstorming process:

1. Problem formulation. Write the formulation of the problem and the four game rules on a black board or flip-chart in such a way that it is visible for everyone. Bring the problem up for discussion once again.
2. Generate and write ideas down. Ask the team members to generate as many ideas as possible and let them raise their hands if they want to share an idea. If

necessary, allow them to share their ideas by turn. Every member should be given the same opportunity to share ideas in the group (as concrete and concise as possible). These ideas have to be written down immediately on a flip-chart or blackboard, in clear sight of all team members. The facilitator should make sure that every member gets a chance to speak. It is not allowed to criticize, discuss or judge ideas. Nobody should be allowed to dominate. While writing down ideas, they should not be amended. Respect for each other's ideas is necessary. Privacy should be guaranteed in such a way that every member can openly share his/her ideas. Stimulate building on ideas of others. Give preference to members who have an idea that builds upon an already mentioned idea. Continue this process until no more ideas are generated. Often, this process lasts up to forty-five minutes.

3. Group and cluster similar ideas.
4. Establish selection criteria e.g. feasibility, costs and relevance.
5. Appoint a group for each cluster of ideas to evaluate the ideas after ending the brainstorming session. Let the groups organize separate follow-up meetings to eliminate unusable ideas themselves on the basis of the selection criteria.
6. Let separate groups work out the ideas and report these to management.

3.2.2 Affinity diagram

What is it?

An affinity diagram is a tool to group a large amount of ideas generated by means of brainstorming.

When do you use it?

An affinity diagram is used on the one hand to group a large amount of ideas based on existing relationships between these ideas, and on the other hand to stimulate creativity and teamwork during the brainstorming process.

How do you use it?

Steps for drafting an affinity diagram:

1. Problem formulation. Write down the problem formulation on a black board or flip-chart in such a way, that it is visible to everyone.
2. The facilitator should allow everyone to formulate their ideas in random order (clearly and concretely in four to seven words, consisting of at least a noun and a verb), and to write them down on a yellow (post-it) note. These notes are then placed in random order on the black board or a large table.
3. When all the ideas/notes have been placed on the board, all team members should come in front to group or categorize the notes around certain themes

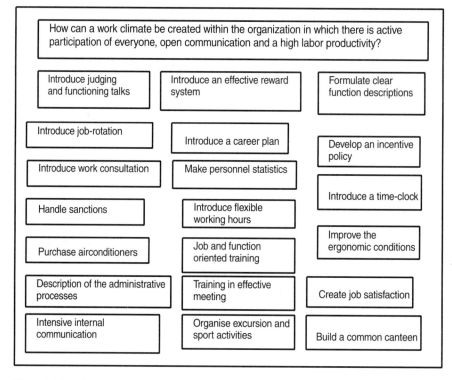

How can a work climate be created within the organization in which there is active participation of everyone, open communication and a high labor productivity?

Introduce judging and functioning talks	Introduce an effective reward system	Formulate clear function descriptions
Introduce job-rotation	Introduce a career plan	Develop an incentive policy
Introduce work consultation	Make personnel statistics	Introduce a time-clock
Handle sanctions	Introduce flexible working hours	Improve the ergonomic conditions
Purchase airconditioners	Job and function oriented training	
Description of the administrative processes	Training in effective meeting	Create job satisfaction
Intensive internal communication	Organise excursion and sport activities	Build a common canteen

Figure 3.9 Step B

without discussion or comments. Group the notes by assumed associations and limit these to ten. In case a note is not in the right place, move it.

4. Place a header above each cluster of notes.

Example

To improve the motivation and labor productivity of the employees, the management of a company organized a brainstorming session using the affinity diagram.

A) An improvement team was put together which formulated the following problem: *"How can a work climate be created within the organization in which there is active participation of everyone, open communication and a high labor productivity?"*

B) On the basis of the already mentioned brainstorming rules, the team members generated some ideas, whereby each idea was written on a yellow (post-it) note, and placed in random order on the board. This board is shown in figure 3.9.

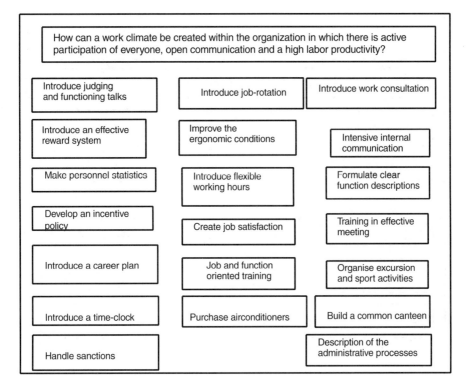

Figure 3.10 Step C

C) Next, all participants were called to the front and they clustered the notes without discussions or comments (see figure 3.10). They also moved the incorrectly placed notes.

D) The previous step resulted in the following clusters of ideas:
- judging/remuneration;
- working conditions;
- communication.

A header was placed above each cluster of notes, as shown in figure 3.11. For each cluster a group was then put together which arranged the ideas according to their priority. The ideas with the highest priority were worked out more accurately by the groups concerned and then reported to the management. In between, plenary attunement meetings were organized to establish synergy between the three groups.

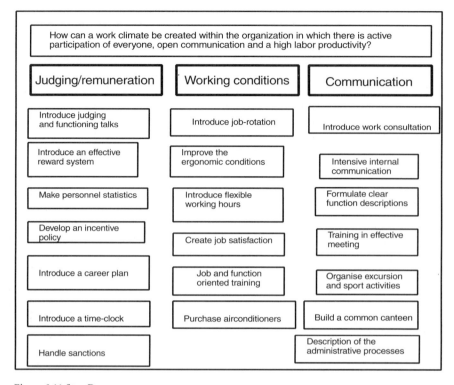

Figure 3.11 Step D

3.2.3 Benchmarking

What is it?

Benchmarking is the systematic and continuous process of determining what the best performances and underlying skills of leading organizations are in their strive for excellence, and based on this, stimulate the organization's own strive for excellent performances at all organizational levels (Camp, 1995). It is a strategy to stimulate changes and optimize performances.

When do you use it?

Benchmarking is mostly used to compare processes and performances against those of recognized leaders. Based on this, the performance gap between the organization and the best competitor is evaluated. Organizational processes usually used for benchmarking are: marketing, sales, purchasing, technology development, product development and logistics. Depending on the chosen subject, several types of benchmarking can be identified (Rampersad, 1997): *Internal, competitive, process, and strategic benchmarking.*

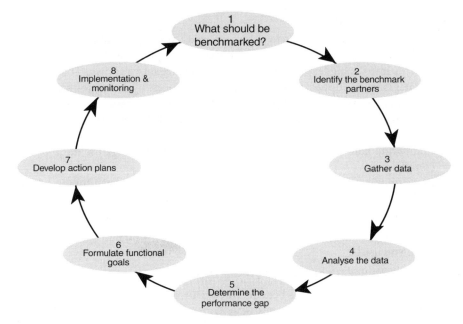

Figure 3.12 The Benchmark process

Internal benchmarking
Internal benchmarking involves a comparison of internal units (activities and processes) within the own company. This is usually of interest to large organizations where it is determined in how far other departments and divisions execute similar activities within their own department more efficiently and effectively.

Competitive benchmarking
During competitive benchmarking, a comparison is made with direct competitors. Operations processes of these competitors are measured and compared against its own situation. Based on what is done by the competitor and what is lacking within the own organization, the own processes can be adjusted to improve efficiency, and thus produce a better and cheaper product. For example; A software producer who wants to improve his competitive position can try to figure out what Microsoft has done to become the market leader.

Process benchmarking
Process benchmarking involves a search for the best in class of a certain process, regardless if it is a competitor or not and in which industrial branch it is applicable. In this way, for example, the logistical activities of a chemical company can be compared with an electronics company with an excellent logistical process.

Strategic benchmarking
Strategic benchmarking is used to obtain sweeping break-throughs in the areas of productivity and distinctive capacity, in order to strengthen its competitive position. This implies big leaps, which are hard to realize on your own. This type of benchmarking can support the strategic planning process by determining the relative competitive position of all business activities and accordingly, suggest the best course to follow. This form of benchmarking can be done in several ways, for example by:
- Comparing your own strategy and financial performance against those of the competitors.
- Determining from the strengths and weaknesses of the competitors in which areas your organization can outdo these competitors, and which improvements are best contributed to its own core competencies.

How do you use it?

Steps for executing the benchmark process (figure 3.12):
1. Determine what should be benchmarked. During this stage, it is determined which functions, tasks, processes, or activities within the own organization will be subjected to benchmarking. Based on the critical success factors (factors that are of decisive importance to the organization, see chapter 9) one or more processes will be selected for benchmarking. Appoint a team that will map these processes in details: identify process stages and determine the process flow, the procedure for each process stage, relevant performance indicators, inputs and outputs of the process and customer requirements. In this stage, the project goals will also be formulated, the data to be collected will be determined, and a tentative list of questions will be prepared.
2. Identify the benchmark partners. Against who should benchmarking be done? Important criteria for the selection of benchmark partners are for instance: the partners should be outstanding (best in class) regarding the benchmark subject, competitiveness of activities, availability of reliable information about the partners. Identifying benchmark partners requires consultation of several information sources such as databases, professional magazines, newspapers, bank reports, annual reports of competitors, seminars, consultancy bureaus, universities etc. In addition, interviews with customers, suppliers, employees, and bankers can be a valuable contribution.
3. Gather data. Data about the process performances of partners are gathered based on interviews, surveys, and consultation of contacts and technical magazines. The process and underlying working methods of partners are examined thoroughly, performance indicators are measured and qualitative and quantitative data are gathered.
4. Analyze the data.
5. Determine the gap between the performance level of the organization and that of its benchmark partner. After the data is gathered, measured, and analyzed,

these will be compared to the data of the own organization. Based on this, the current performance gap between the own organization and that of the benchmark partner is determined. The differences in underlying working methods and the causes of the differences in performance will also be documented. The main question is: Why are the efficiency and effectiveness of the own process lagging behind that of the best in class?

6. Formulate functional goals. Based on the results of the benchmark-study, new functional goals will be formulated to close the performance gap. The benchmark results should also be integrated into the company's policy to facilitate the implementation of the improvement possibilities.

7. Develop action plans. The goals should now be transformed into concrete action plans. These plans should provide an explanation about the following questions: When should which action with which goal be implemented? How can changes successfully be implemented? Who does what? In which way? Who is responsible for the implementation of the different actions?

8. Implement specific actions and monitor the progress. This step relates to the execution of improvement actions and introduction of changes. The continuation of the implementation should be checked constantly for successful execution, verified whether the actions are executed as planned, whether the process is in fact changing (with which results), and if the benchmark goals are being met. Based on this, possible adjustments will be made.

9. Start again. Benchmarking is not a one-time activity, but a process of continuous improvement. There are always other and better improvement methods. Competition is not standing idle, in due time new best practices are developed.

Example

As an example, a statement from one of the managers of Rank Xerox Netherlands (Prins, 1997) is used.

"In the past, the order processing department of Rank Xerox had 20 employees, whereby the throughput time of an invoice was 5 to 8 days. After a benchmark-study, the activities within the department were divided into four segments based on the invoice amount. Finally, the number of persons in the department was reduced and an invoice was send within 24 hours for 95% of the orders. The reason for the benchmark-study was that customers were displeased about the long delivery time. Finally, a shorter delivery time also resulted in an acceleration of the invoicing, a smaller department, a higher customer satisfaction and a swift payment of the claims or an improvement of the liquidity".

B. Van Saase, Director Quality & Customer Satisfaction, Rank Xerox Netherlands.

3.2.4 Fishbone diagram

What is it?

A fishbone diagram or Ishikawa-diagram is a graphic representation of the relationship between a given effect and its potential causes (Ishikawa, 1985). The potential causes are divided into categories and sub-categories so that the display resembles a skeleton of a fish.

When do you use it?

A fishbone diagram (also known as a cause-and-effect diagram) is used to analyze cause-and-effect relationships and based on this, facilitate the search for solutions of related problems. It is a useful tool in brainstorming, process evaluation, and planning activities.

How do you use it?

Steps for drafting a fishbone diagram:
1. Define the effect clearly and concisely. Place a short description of this in a box and draw from this box a long line to the left.
2. Determine during brainstorming sessions the most important categories of causes. Possible categories of causes are:
   - equipment;
   - working methods;
   - environment;
   - organization;
   - materials; raw materials, semi-manufactured articles, energy, data and information.
   - people; knowledge, skills, attitude, style and behavior.
   - means; facilities.
   - management; knowledge, skills, attitude, style and behavior.
   - information;
   - measurements.
3. Place these categories with some distance between them along the main line (see figure 3.13)
4. Draw skew lines from these categories to the main line.
5. Look during brainstorming for a couple of possible causes and place these on the diagram by the corresponding category; doing this also for the subsequent levels, will result in branching. A good rule of thumb is to repeat the question "why" five times.
6. Judge and analyze the possible causes.
7. Select a small number (3 to 5) of highest-level causes that are likely to have the greatest influence on the effect.
8. Look for possible solutions for these causes.
9. Introduce the changes.

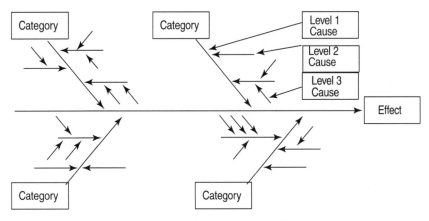

Development of cause-and-effect diagram

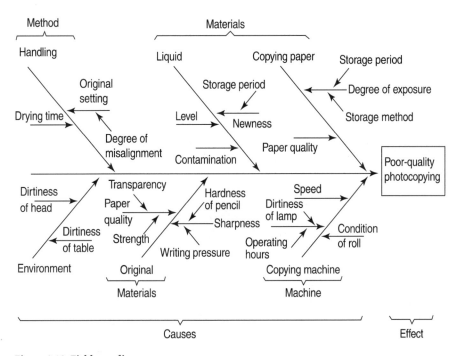

Figure 3.13: Fishbone diagram

Example

A copying company receives a lot of complaints about poor quality photocopies. Management decides to analyze this problem through a fishbone diagram. Figure 3.13 shows the different causes that are identified (NEN-ISO 9004-4, 1993).

3.2.5 Check sheet

What is it?

A check sheet is a form for systematic data gathering and registering to get a clear view of the facts. It is used to keep track of how often something occurs. A check sheet offers the possibility for everyone to register similar data in the same way.

When do you use it?

A check sheet is used to indicate the frequency of a certain occurrence.

How do you use it?

Steps for drafting a data sheet:
1. Formulate the objective for collecting data.
2. Decide which data is necessary.
3. Determine who and how data will be analyzed.
4. Develop a list on which everyone participating with the study can record the collected data.
5. Start counting by tallying on the list; I, II, III, IIII, and IIIII represent the numbers 1,2,3,4,and 5, respectively.
6. Indicate on the list the total number of facts, which were noticed.

Example

A copying company notices a sudden increase in complaints about poor quality photocopies. Management decides to analyze these complaints by using a check sheet to trace the causes (table 3.1).

Table 3.1: Types of defects

Causes of defects	Types of defects				Data collected by: John Adams Date: October 11, 2000 Total
	Missing pages	Muddy copies	Pages out of sequence	Show through	
Humidity	II	IIIII III		I	11
Machine jams		II		I	3
Toner	III	II	I	II	8
Conditions of originals	I	II	IIIII I	I	10
Total	6	14	7	5	32

3.2.6 Flow chart

What is it?

A flow chart clearly shows the steps of a process, by using standard symbols. It allows you to examine and understand relationships in a process.

When do you use it?

A flow chart is used to document and analyze the connection and sequence of events in a process. It is used to create an integrated understanding of the activities that are performed and the relationship between the different process steps.

How do you use it?

Steps for drafting a flow chart:

1. Decide which process should be mapped.
2. Clearly define the borders of this process.
3. Define the start and end of the process.
4. Define the steps in the process; determine the activities, decisions, inputs and outputs of the process.
5. Map the process using standard symbols (see figure 3.14): also draw eventual feedback loops in the chart and check that each process step doesn't have more than one output.
6. Compare the flow chart with the actual process.
7. Date the flow chart for future reference and use.

The start or end of the flow chart: START   END

A rectangle indicates a process or activity:

A diamond indicates a decision:

Arrows show the direction or flow of the process:

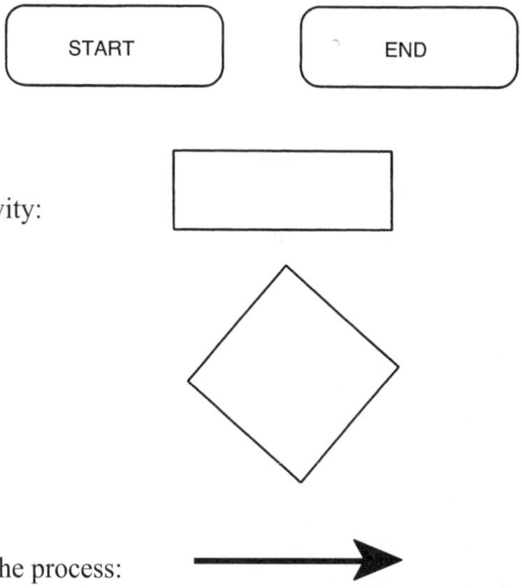

Figure 3.14 Standard symbols used for drafting flow charts

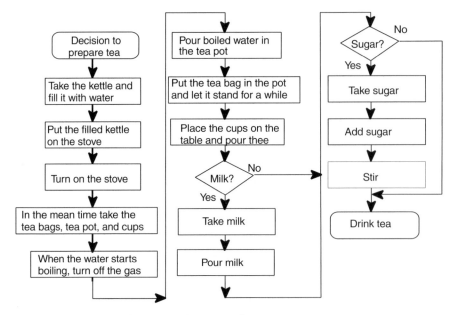

Figure 3.15 A flowchart of the process "serving tea"

Example

Figure 3.15 illustrates a flow chart of the process "serving tea". It's one of the many possible flow charts of this process.

3.2.7 Line graph

What is it?

A line graph is a graphic representation of the relationship between two variables. It is a communication tool which represents data in simple graphical form that is quickly and easily understood.

When do you use it?

A line graph is used to visualize the relationship between two variables and to study fluctuations in time. Line graphs are particularly used to identify trends in a certain process.

How do you use it?

Steps for drawing a graph:

1. Draw a vertical (Y) and a horizontal (X) axis and label both axes. Usually, the time sequence is indicated on the horizontal axis (year, weak, hour etc.).

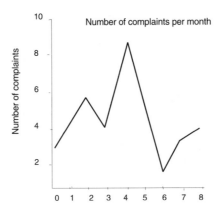

Figure 3.16 Line graph

2. Choose a scale so that most of the available space is filled by the graph. Both axes usually start at zero.
3. Plot the different points in the graph and draw straight lines in the correct sequence between the points.
4. Give the graph a clear descriptive title.

Example

Figure 3.16 shows a line graph illustrating the number of complaints from customers over the last 8 months. This shows that most of the complaints were received in month 4 and the least in month 6.

3.2.8 Run chart

What is it?

A run chart encompasses a kind of time series graph to monitor a process.

When do you use it?

A run chart is used to identify trends and significant changes in a process.

How do you use it?

Steps for drawing a run chart:

1. Collect the necessary data.
2. Draw a vertical (Y) and a horizontal (X) axis; usually the points of time are marked out on the X-axis.
3. Plot the data in the graph and draw a straight line between these points.

4. Check if there are developments, trends and changes. A trend is a series of points, which display an upward or downward slope.

Example

The manager of a jeweller shop in Brussels notices that there are periods where he cannot handle the demand. There are also periods in which he hardly has anything to do. He decides to study which fluctuations in sales occur during one year, to identify the peaks and lows. He hopes to forecast the queue in the shop better with this tool. To do this, he collects the following data (see table 3.2), which he marks out on a run chart (see figure 3.17).

Table 3.2 Collected data

Month	Sales (x $ 5000)	Month	Sales (x $ 5000)
January	2	July	4.5
February	6.5	August	3
March	4.5	September	5.5
April	9	October	6
May	5.5	November	6.5
June	4	December	11

The run chart displays an interesting pattern. There are peaks in February (Valentines Day), April (Easter) and December (Christmas). The least are sold in January because people have to be conscious about expenses after the holidays and in August when many are on vacation.

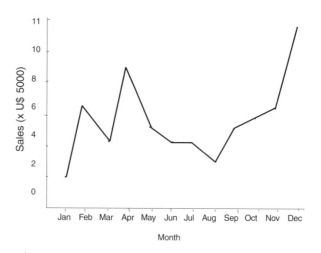

Figure 3.17 Run chart

3.2.9 Histogram

What is it?

A histogram is a bar diagram, which indicates how data is divided in a group of values. Such a display is also known as a frequency distribution. The data are displayed as a series of rectangles of equal width and varying heights. An examination of the patterns of varying heights offers insight into process behavior.

When do you use it?

A histogram is used to clearly show where the most frequently occurring values are located and how the data is distributed. It is also a tool for determining the maximum process results. Based on the visual information about process behavior, priorities can be set about the improvement efforts.

How do you use it?

Steps for drafting a histogram:

1. After the necessary measurements are taken, count how many data values you have gathered.
2. Determine the range of the data by subtracting the lowest values from the highest.
3. Divide the data values in groups or classes and count the number of values in each class. Follow the guidelines that are shown in table 3.3.

Table 3.3 Guide lines

Number of values	Number of classes
Less than 50	5 – 7
50-100	6 – 10
100-250	7 – 12
More than 250	10 – 20

Thus, if you have gathered 110 data values, you can distribute those over a minimum of 7 and a maximum of 12 classes.

4. Then, determine the width of the classes by:
   - dividing the range by the minimal number of classes;
   - dividing the range by the maximal number of classes;
   - choose a class width that is somewhere between the two results.
5. Make a frequency table for all values.
6. Draw a histogram based on the frequency table. Mark the class limits on the horizontal axis and the frequency on the vertical axis.
7. Write the title and number of values in the empty spaces of the diagram.

Example

The Human Resource manager of an organization decides to study how long it takes to recruit administrative employees, from the moment the vacancy is known till the day the new employee is hired. He studies the files of his department and registers how many working days the procedure took (PA Consulting Group, 1991).

> Time spent recruiting new employees (in working days):
> 32 27 27 36 31 31 19 38 12 28 25 33 48 44 16 34 21 28 27 59 31 31 39 36 57 53 29 36 47 39 26 41 34 38
> 42 41 13 22 37 21 27 31 21 29 24 29 17 18 26 22 19 33 26 32 21

Next, he makes the following calculations:
Number of data values = 55
Range = 59 – 12 = 47

The class width lies between 7.8 (47 divided by 6) and 4.7 (47 divided by 10). The choice is a class width of 5. Next, he drafts a frequency table, (see table 3.4.). Based on this, he draws the corresponding histogram, see figure 3.18.

Table 3.4 Frequency table

Class	Limits	Counts	Frequency
1	10 – 14	||	2
2	15 – 19	̶H̶l̶	5
3	20 – 24	̶H̶l̶ ||	7
4	25 – 29	̶H̶l̶ ̶H̶l̶ |||	13
5	30 – 34	̶H̶l̶ ̶H̶l̶ |	11
6	35 – 39	̶H̶l̶ |||	8
7	40 – 44	||||	4
8	45 – 49	||	2
9	50 – 54	|	1
10	55 – 59	||	2
		Total :	55

The histogram indicates that most recruitment procedures take 25 to 29 days (class 4).

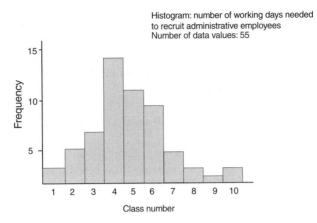

Figure 3.18 Histogram

3.2.10 Pareto-diagram

What is it?

A Pareto-diagram is a graphical tool to gain insight into the most important causes of a problem. It is a bar chart in which the data are arranged in descending order of their importance; the diagram displays the relative contribution of each item to the total effect in decreasing order. Based on this, the most important problems can be distinguished from the less important ones and the greatest improvement can be realized with the least effort. The diagram is based on the Pareto-principle, which states that just a few of the defects account for most of the effects. This pattern is called the 80/20-rule and is applicable to all sorts of situations; thus, it is likely that only 20 percent of your equipment problems account for 80 percent of the downtime. The issue here is that of many problems, only a limited number are essential and should be solved immediately. The rest can be solved later. A Pareto-diagram clearly indicates which problems belong to this small number. Interpretation of the diagram should be done with care, because the most frequent occurring problems are usually not the most expensive ones.

When do you use it?

A Pareto-diagram is used to systematically organize collected data. Based on this, the most important causes of a problem and priorities can be identified. It aids the decision-making process because it puts the most critical issues into an easily understood framework.

How do you use it?

Steps for drafting a Pareto-diagram:

1. Formulate the problem.

2. Select the time-period during which an inventory of its causes should be made.
3. Design a check sheet for registering the gathered data.
4. Make an inventory of the causes. Count the number of times each cause occurs and write it down on the check sheet.
5. Calculate the total.
6. Rank the causes in decreasing order. If necessary, the category "others" can be used here.
7. Draw a bar chart with two vertical axes. Along the left vertical axis, mark the measured values for each cause, starting from zero till the total number of causes. The right vertical axis should have the same height and should go from 0 to 100%. This axis displays the cumulative percentages. List the different kinds of causes along the horizontal axis, from left to right in decreasing order of frequency or costs.
8. Draw a bar above each item whose height represents the number for that cause.
9. Construct the cumulative frequency line. First draw the cumulative bars by adding the number of each cause from left to right. Then draw a cumulative curved line from zero till the 100% level on the right vertical axis, by connecting the top right hand corner of the bars with each other.
10. Draw a horizontal line from 80% (on the right vertical axis) to the left till the point of intersection with the cumulative line, and then draw a vertical line from this intersection downwards till the horizontal axis. Left from this intersection point, 20% of the causes are located (the most essential bottlenecks) causing 80% of the damages. Thus, causes which require immediate attention.

Example 1

The manager of a hotel is concerned about the number of complaints he receives from customers. That's why he has decided to study the most important problems, in order to initiate corrective measures. With the help of his employees, he drafts a check sheet with all known problems for each separate department. During the following four weeks, the employees register the complaints. They use the check sheets shown in table 3.5 (PA Consulting Group, 1991). The corresponding Pareto-diagram is shown in figure 3.19. During the period studied, 40 complaints were registered. From the Pareto-diagram, it appears that 80 % of the complaints relate to only 5 of the 23 possible causes. These are, ranked according to priorities: "slow service in the restaurant", "coffee arrives too late in the conference room ", "bedrooms are not clean", "restaurant personnel is impolite", "noisy rooms". These complaints should be solved first.

Table 3.5 Data sheets collection

Restaurant		Conference room	
Types of complaints	**Number of complaints**	**Types of complaints**	**Number of complaints**
Cold food		Defective equipment	
Slow service	⊮⊮ ⊮⊮	Coffee too late	⊮⊮ ⊮⊮
Expensive		Too few provisions	
Cork parts in the wine		Too cold	│
Overcooked food		Impolite personnel	│
Impolite personnel	‖‖		

Recreation center		Bedrooms	
Types of complaints	**Number of complaints**	**Types of complaints**	**Number of complaints**
Hygiene		Beds not made	
Unavailable facilities	‖	Too cold	
Cold swimming water		Not clean	⊮ │
Too crowded		TV's not working	
Defective equipment		No towels	│
Impolite personnel	│	Noisy	‖‖

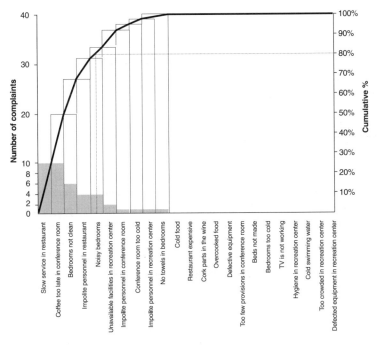

Figure 3.19 Pareto-diagram

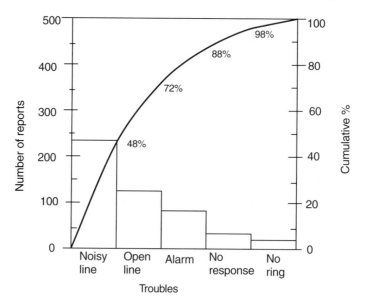

Figure 3.20 Pareto-diagram for reports of troubles with telephones

Example 2

Figure 3.20 represents a Pareto-diagram for reports of troubles with telephones (NEN-ISO 9004-4, 1993). This diagram shows that noisy lines and open lines account for 72% of the telephone-trouble reports, and that these indicate the greatest opportunities for improvement.

3.2.11 Failure Mode and Effect Analysis

What is it?

Failure Mode and Effect Analysis (FMEA), also known as risk analysis, is a preventive measure to systematically display the causes, effects, and possible actions regarding observed failures. FMEA is usually used to analyze products and processes (Rampersad, 1996). In this book the emphasis is on processes (process FMEA). Answers to the following questions are sought here in advance for each process step: How can process execution fail? What are the possible causes of this? What happens if the process execution fails? And how can we prevent this?

When do you use it?

Process FMEA is used to systematically identify failures in the process and to eliminate them. These result in a list of critical points, with instructions on what should be done to minimize the chance of process failure.

How do you use it?

The execution of FMEA is based on teamwork. The chairperson is responsible for: forming a team, gathering relevant information, organizing and planning the FMEA session(s), leading the discussions, registering the results, and providing feedback regarding the improvements. To identify as many problems as possible, the team should have a multidisciplinary and broad composition with team members who have extensive experience in their field of expertise. A session should take 1.5 hours at the most, depending on the formulation of the problem, the knowledge and experience of the team members, and preparation of the session.

Steps for implementation of a FMEA (Rampersad, 1996):
The chairperson should:
1. Form a multidisciplinary and expert team of 5 to 8 members.
2. Call a brief meeting beforehand and explain the objective of the session, the FMEA approach, and their role to the team members.
3. Make relevant information available to the team members; these should be thoroughly studied in advance by the team members.
4. Make an inventory of all relevant process steps.

During the session (while completing the FMEA-forms):
5. Determine for each process step the possible failure modes. Thus, anticipate possible failures in the process, and in relation to the other process steps (see table 3.7).
6. Indicate what the cause is of each failure mode.
7. Indicate what the effect is on the controllability of the process.
8. Quantify the weak points in the process, by estimating the Probability of occurrence (P) and the Severity of the failure (S) for each failure mode (see table 3.6). The product of these two factors is the Risk Priority Number (RPN). The chance of discovering the error on time is expressed in the factor S. The more difficult it is to discover the error in advance, the higher this factor will be.

Table 3.6. Factor P and factor S

Factor P	Factor S
De *factor P* can be determined with the following scale: 0 = not possible/ never 1 = very low 2 = low 3 = not as low 4 = less then average 5 = average 6 = above average 7 = rather high 8 = high 9 = very high 10 = certain	De *factor S* can be scaled as follows: 0 = no problem 1 = very low/hardly any problem 2 = low/to be solved through intervention of the employee 3 = less serious 4 = less then average 5 = average 6 = above average 7 = rather serious 8 = high 9 = very high 10 = catastrophic/dangerous to people

9. Determine for each failure mode the actions necessary to improve the weak points in the process. The failures with the highest RPN factors have the highest priority.
10. Appoint a responsible problem solver to solve the highest risk cases.
11. Agree on a period in time for verification of the solutions.

Afterward:

12. Report the FMEA results in writing to management.
13. Give feedback to the team members about the status of the executed actions.
14. Verify and evaluate the actions.

Table 3.7 Failure Mode and Effect Analysis

Date: Oct. 2000 Page: 1	Company: Johnson Furniture Department : Operations Main process: Manufacturing of chairs	Team members: Rita, Rodney, Warren, William, David Prepared by: Rodney							
Process steps	Failure mode	Cause	Effect	P	S	RPN	Action	Responsible	Date
Supply logs	Difficult to supply Danger to personnel	No adequate transport and handling equipment available	Production delay	7	10	70	Provide adequate transport and handling system	David	November 2000
Sort logs	Logs are falling from the sorting band	Wrong construction of the rolling band	Production stagnation	5	7	35	Redesign the rolling band	Rodney	December 2000
Saw logs	Difficult to saw	Logs are too big for the sawing machine.	Damage to the sawing machine	6	5	30	Optimize the selection process	Warren	January 2001
		A wrong saw blade was assembled in the sawing machine	Bad sawing quality	2	4	8	-	-	-
Drill boards	Drilling machine regularly defective	Maintenance system is not adequate	Production delays	8	5	40	Develop and implement a preventive maintenance system	Rita	February 2001
Scour board	Danger to personnel due to dust development	Insufficient extraction of dust	High absence due to illness	5	10	50	Install a dust extraction system	Rodney	December 2000

Example

A producer of wooden furniture regularly receives a lot of complaints from customers about too late deliveries of chairs. Based on this, management decided to analyze the problems within the organization. After a detailed study, manufacturing chairs (within Operations) appears to be the most critical process of the company. That is why a decision is made to limit the analysis to this process. This process is then divided into the following process steps: supply logs, sort logs, saw logs, drill boards and scour boards. Then the team determined the failures, causes, effects, and possible actions (see table 3.7).

3.2.12 Scatter diagram

What is it?

A scatter diagram is a graphical technique for studying relationships between two variables (which occur in pairs) to figure out if there is a connection between the variables and how strong this relationship is. The diagram displays the paired data as a cloud of points. Relationships between the two variables are inferred from the shape of the clouds. The density and direction of the cloud indicate how the two variables influence each other. If the value of one variable seems to influence the other, then there is a correlation between these two variables. A positive relationship between two variables means that increasing values of one variable are associated with increasing values of the other. A negative relationship on the other hand, means that increasing values of one variable are associated with decreasing values of the other. Six commonly occurring shapes of clouds are shown in figure 3.21 (NEN-ISO 9004-4, 1993).

When do you use it?

A scatter diagram is used after a cause and effect analysis to determine whether a certain cause is related to a certain effect. This can be used to determine what will happen to the one variable if the other is changed.

How do you use it?

Steps for drafting a scatter diagram:
1. Collect 30 to 50 paired data of two associated sets of variables (cause and effect) whose relationship is to be studied.
2. Draw a horizontal (X) and a vertical (Y) axis. Usually the values related to the cause are marked on the X-axis and those related to the effect on the Y-axis. Both axes should approximately be of equal length.
3. Label the axes, give the diagram a title and register the data source, date and the responsible persons.
4. Plot the paired (x, y) data in the diagram, by marking each point. When pairs of data have the same values, draw a concentric circle round these points.
5. Examine the shape of the cloud of points in the diagram to determine the type and strength of the mutual relationships.

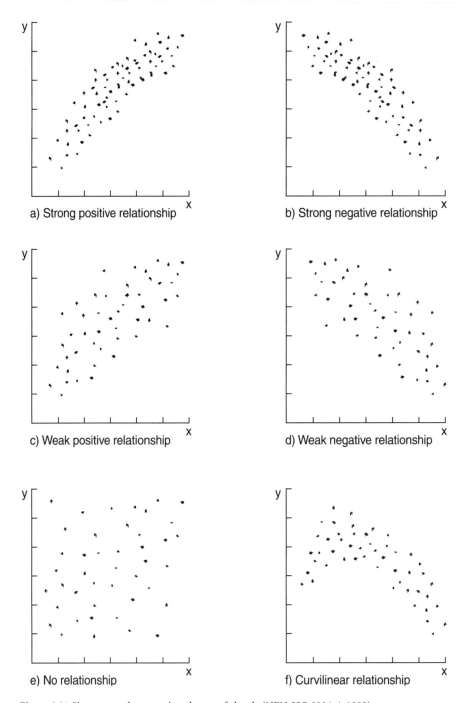

Figure 3.21 Six commonly occurring shapes of clouds (NEN-ISO 9004-4, 1993)

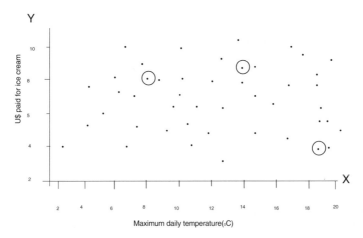

Figure 3.22 Scatter diagram

Example

The manager of Florence Ice Cream in New York receives an interesting offer from an ice cream supplier. The supplier introduces a new kind of ice cream on the market, which was tested on the market with positive results. The profits from the new ice cream seem promising. If Florence orders a sufficient amount of the new ice cream, a new freezer must be installed. It is known that the tests were done during warm weather and Florence is afraid that the new ice cream will not sell as well when it is cold. That is why the company decided to study the relationship between the sale of ice cream and the maximum daily temperature. Each day during four weeks, the company registered the sales data and compared these with the temperature measured that day. The scatter diagram derived from this is shown in figure 3.22.

From the diagram, it appears that there is little connection between ice cream sales and the maximum daily temperature. Based on this, Florence can decide to install a second freezer and stock the new ice cream, possibly after also studying the effects of other factors on sales. Thus, decision making was made possible with help of the scatter diagram.

3.2.13 Control chart

What is it?

A control chart is a graph that displays data taken over time and the variations of this data. It is a tool to determine the difference between variations in a process as a result of demonstrable causes and variations that happen by chance. The control chart indicates what a process can do. This can be used to check whether the process is being controlled statistically. The control chart is based on a series of random samples taken at regular intervals, and shows to what extent process performance is subject to variations. The control chart can be divided into two categories:

– Control chart of variables; for measurable data such as time, length, temperature, weight, pressure, etc.
– Control chart of characteristics; for quantifiable data such as number of defects, typing errors in a report, etc.

When do you use it?

A control chart is used to show the most important sources of variations (destabilizing factors) and to eliminate them in order to statistically control the process. It allows you to distinguish between measurements which are predictable (related to the inherent capability of the process) and measurements which are unpredictable (produced by special causes). The chart is used to evaluate process stability and to decide when to adjust the process. There are many kinds of control charts, but it depends on the situation which type of control chart is used. In this book, emphasis is placed on the Moving Range control chart for individual measurements of process parameters (variables). It is a combined chart for the position and spread of the quality parameters. The most important conditions for using this frequently applied chart are (Does, 1996):

• the measurements are completed in a continuous scale;
• the random samples are independent of each other;
• the measurements are approximately normally distributed.

How do you use it?

Steps for making a control chart:
1. Select the characteristics for applying a control chart.
2. Select the appropriate type of control chart.
3. Collect the data.
4. Draw a vertical axis (Y-axis) with the value of the quality characteristic (e.g. time, length, etc.). The position (spread) of the quality parameters of the process is shown on this axis.
5. Draw a horizontal axis (X-axis) with the time of measurement or samples taken at random.
6. Draw the central line (CL) which is the average of the process, with on each side (see figure 3.23):
   • the Lower Control Limit (LCL);
   • the Upper Control Limit (UCL).
   These limits describe the natural variation of the process.
7. Plot the data in the chart.
8. Examine the plot for points outside the control limits. Points under the Lower Control Limit or above the Upper Control Limit signal that something has occurred which requires special attention. The circled point on the chart in figure 3.23 is outside the Upper Control Limit. This point is a sign for a corrective action.

The individual measurements X_1, X_2, X_3, etc. form the basis of the Moving Range control chart. Thus, X_1 is the value of the first measurement. The central line (CL) or the average of k measurements can be calculated as follows:

$$CL = \frac{(X_1 + X_2 + X_3 + \ldots + X_k)}{k}$$

$$CL = \frac{1}{k}\sum_{t=1}^{k} X_t$$

The Upper Control Limit and the Lower Control Limit (for more than 10 measurements) can be calculated as follows:

$$UCL = CL + 2{,}66\ MR$$

$$LCL = CL - 2{,}66\ MR$$

$$MR = \frac{1}{k-1}\sum_{t=2}^{k} \left| X_t - X_{t-1} \right|$$

MR is the average Moving Range; a measurement for the spread of the average random samples. The constant figure 2,66 is used here to determine the distance between the central line and the control borders.

Example

To check if an assembled machine is in good working condition, and to evaluate the stability of the assembly process, an employee measures the time to complete a certain task for 20 individually mounted machines. These figures are given in table 3.8 (Does, 1996).

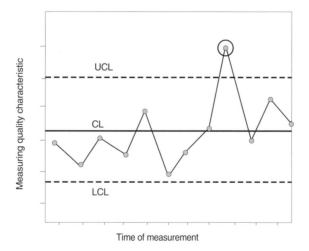

Figure 3.23 Example of a control chart

Table 3.8 Measurement values

Machine	Time (sec)	$\lvert X_t - X_{t-1} \rvert$	Machine	Time (sec)	$\lvert X_t - X_{t-1} \rvert$
1	2.12	-	11	3.69	1.34
2	1.81	0.31	12	2.10	1.59
3	1.93	0.12	13	2.05	0.05
4	3.46	1.53	14	2.60	0.55
5	3.50	0.04	15	1.88	0.72
6	2.25	1.25	16	2.28	0.40
7	2.44	0.19	17	2.90	0.62
8	2.85	1.40	18	1.40	0.50
9	1.75	1.10	19	1.90	0.50
10	2.35	0.60	20	3.60	1.70
			Average	2.24	0.76

$$CL = \frac{1}{k}\sum_{t=1}^{k} X_t \ (k=20)$$

So: CL = $(X_1 + X_2 + X_3 +\ldots\ldots+ X_{20})$ / 20
  CL = [2.12 + 1.81 + 1.93 + 3.46 +\ldots\ldots\ldots+ 1.90 + 3.60] / 20 = 2.24

$$MR = \frac{1}{k-1}\sum_{t=2}^{k} \lvert X_t - X_{t-1} \rvert$$

So: $MR = \frac{1}{19}\sum_{t=2}^{20} \lvert X_t - X_{t-1} \rvert$

MR = [0.31 + 0.12 + 1.53 + 0.04 +\ldots\ldots\ldots+ 0.50 + 1.70] / 19 = 0.76

UCL = CL + 2,66 MR = 2.24 + 2.66 x 0.76 = 4.46

LCL = CL – 2,66 MR = 2.24 – 2.66 x 0.76 = 0.42

Figure 3.24 shows that the measurement values are within the control limits. The assembly process is statistically controlled and there is therefore no reason to take action.

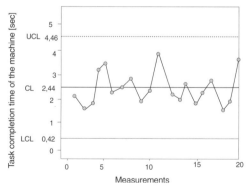

Figure 3.24 Control chart of the assembly process

3.2.14 Quality Function Deployment

What is it?

Quality Function Deployment (QFD) is a method to systematically and structurally convert customer's wishes in an early stage into critical aspects of your product, service and/or process. In this original Japanese approach, the customer's wishes are confronted with the help of matrices, with detailed technical parameters and project objectives (figure 3.25). Because of this form, the figure is called the quality house. The critical product specifications (technical parameters) are translated in detail, by means of three sequel houses, into the manner in which the process is to be controllably executed, to achieve stable and acceptable product quality (see figure 3.26). In the first house, the link is made between customer wishes and product specifications. In the second house, the relationship between these product specifications and the characteristics of the product parts is central. In the third house, the link is laid between product parts and process characteristics. As a result, the performance indicators of critical processes are established. Finally, the process characteristics are translated in the fourth house into the controlled way manufacturing process operations are to be executed. This results, among other things, in standard working procedures for each process step (Hauser & Clausing, 1988, and Rampersad, 1994). In this book, the emphasis is placed on the first quality house (the relationship between customer's wishes and product specifications).

When do you use it?

QFD is used to better understand the customer and to develop products, services and processes in a more customer-oriented way. The objective of QFD is to allow the "voice of the customer" to be heard more clearly in the product development process and related operational processes, but also to comply with the "do it right the first time" principle.

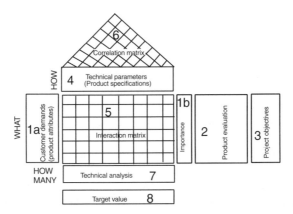

Figure 3.25 Basic structure QFD-diagram

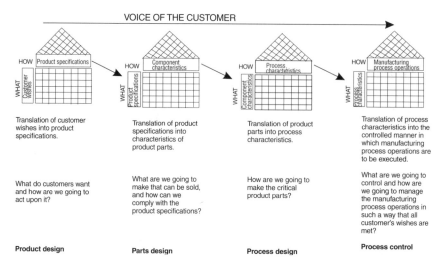

Figure 3.26 Steps within QFD

How do you use it?

Put together a multidisciplinary expert team, which is coached by a team leader and supported by a QFD-facilitator. The team leader should preferably be a product manager or product engineer. The characteristics of the team leader and the team members are more fully explained in chapter 5. The QFD-facilitator is someone who is an expert in the field of QFD. He acts as the source of information and advises the team concerning the effective use of this method. In this preparatory phase, also formulate the objectives and the scope of the QFD-project. Central questions here are: *Is senior management committed? Which important product are we going to improve? For which markets? Who are our customers? Which competing products are we going to compare our products to? How long will project execution take? Which milestones can we distinguish? What does the reporting structure look like?*

Steps for building the first quality house (see figure 3.25):

1. Define the customer, make an inventory of the customer's expectations and measure the priority of these wishes using weighing scores. An inventory can be made of the customer's expectations (product attributes) through interviews, inquiries, etc. Visiting trade shows, experience of salesmen, customer registration, direct contact, contact with the competition among other things, are all important information sources for appraising and mapping the customer's expectations. Benchmarking can be of use here.
2. Compare the performance of your product with that of competitive products. Evaluate your product and note what the strong and weak points are according to the customer.

3. Identify and quantify the improvement objectives. Note which expectations of the customer need to be improved in relationship to the competitive product and indicate this in a score.
4. Translate the customer's expectations into quantifiable technical parameters or product specifications. State how the client's wishes can be used to your advantage. Examples of technical parameters are *dimensions, weight, number of parts, energy use, capacity,* etc.
5. Investigate the relationships between the customer's expectations and the technical parameters. Note in a matrix up to what level the customer's expectations are influenced by the technical parameters and indicate this relationship through a score.
6. Identify the interactions between the technical parameters. Make the relationships between these parameters explicit in the roof of the quality house.
7. Record the measure unit of all technical parameters. Express these parameters in measurable data. For instance, the dimensions of an object are 150 mm (l) x 320 mm (w) x 550 mm (h) and the weight is 15 kg.
8. Determine the target values of the new product design; note the proposed improvements of the technical parameters.

Example

This example entails the design improvement of an attaché case. Figure 3.27 shows the filled in quality house for the improved design of the attaché case based on the customer's expectations (Roozenburg & Eekels, 1995).

Step 1: Establishing the customer's expectations

The customer's expectations are established by means of brainstorming and are classified in the part named 1a of the quality house (see figure 3.25). This step deals with what is important to the customer, such as: *nice to wear, easy to open, easy to fill,* etc. (see figure 3.27). These demands aren't all of equal importance. The importance of these demands is indicated with the help of weight factors (part 1b in figure 3.25). A five-point scale is used here, with: 5 = very important, 4 = important, 3 = less important (but nice to have), 2 = not so important and 1 = not important. Accordingly, the *"easy to carry"* demand has a value of 2 points because it is not so important, and *"durable"* has 5 points because it is very important (see figure 3.27).

Step 2: Product evaluation

In this step, our current product (attaché case) is compared to one or more important competitive products. In this way, insight is gained as to how our product performs compared to that of the competition. In this case, a five-point scale from excellent to poor is used: 5 = excellent, 4 = good, 3 = fairly good, 2 = not so good and 1 = poor. This is indicated in part 2 of the house (see figure 3.27). Here, our

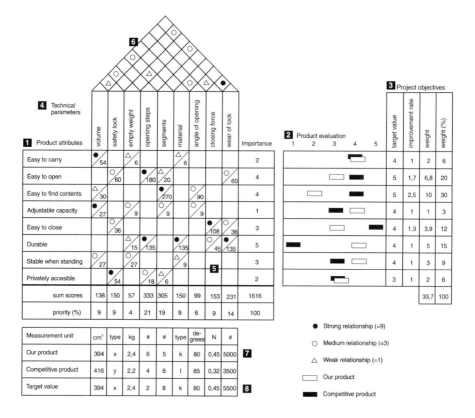

Figure 3.27 A filled in quality house (Roozenburg & Eekels, 1995)

product is shown as a white square and that of the competitor as a black square. Our attaché case was considered more durable and more stable in a standing position than that of the competition. On the other hand, the attaché case of the competition is easier to open and close, and the layout of the interior is more conveniently arranged. As a result, the content is easier to find. This immediately shows the potential for improvement of our product.

Step 3: Project objectives

In this step, the customer's expectations we want to improve in relation to the competitor are indicated. In other words, the target value for each product attribute is indicated through a score (in part 3 of the house). Once again, a five-point scale is used. For the attributes that need no improvement, the target value is put on a par with the current score of the product evaluation. In the project team (by brainstorming), it was decided that the product attributes *"easy to carry"*, *"adjustable capacity"*, *"durability"*, *"stable when standing"* and *"privately accessible"*, did not need improvement. They received a target value of 4, 4, 4, 4, and 3 respectively (they are constant on the same level as shown in figure 3.27). The customer's expectations *"easy to open"* and *"easy to find contents"* which now have a score of respectively 3 and 2 (lower than that of the competition) will be improved to a score of 5 (better than the competition). The wish *"easy to close"* (score 3) will be improved to a score of 4 (small improvement). On the basis of the target value, the improvement rate can now be established.

The improvement rate = target value / evaluation score

From this part of the house, it can be concluded that the QFD-team has decided to improve the opening and closing of the suitcase, and to improve the ease of finding the contents; an improvement rate of 1.7, 1.3, and 2.5 respectively (see figure 3.27). Next, the weight (importance) of each customer's expectation or product attribute is established as a project objective.

The weight = improvement rate x the relevant importance-weight factor

Accordingly, the weight of *"easy to carry"* = 1 x 2 = 2.

The weight of *"easy to open"* = 1.7 x 4 = 6.8.

The weight of *"easy to close"* = 1.3 x 3 = 3.9, etc.

All weights were then added after which the total in the last column was used to calculate the weight in % of each attribute. For example, the weight of the attribute *"easy to carry"* has a percentage value of 6/33.7 x 100% = 6%. *Durability* has a weight percentage of 15/33.7 x 100% = 15%. The total of all weight percentages is 100 (see figure 3.27, part 3).

Step 4: Technical parameters/product specifications

After the activities to visualize the importance of the customer's expectations were finished, it was decided on HOW to handle these expectations. Through brainstorming, it was decided which technical parameters or characteristics are influenced by the different customer expectations. More specifically, the measure in which a HOW (specification) relates to a WHAT (customer's expectation). In this example, nine technical parameters related to the customer's wishes are distinguished, namely: *volume, safety latch, weight when empty,* etc (see part 4 in figure 3.27). The product design is determined by these parameters.

Step 5: Interaction matrix

In this step, the level in which the technical parameters influence the customer's expectations is studied. This is done in the interaction matrix (see part 5 in figure 3.27). In this matrix, the relationships between the customer's expectations or product attributes and technical parameters are being studied. This involves a coupling between WHAT and HOW. An empty row in the matrix means that there is no relationship between the technical product characteristics and the related customer's expectation (the product does not satisfy this need). An empty column points to an unnecessary product characteristic, which is included; making the product too expensive. For each cell of the matrix, it is determined whether there is a relationship between the attributes and parameters, and if so, how strong this relationship is. The following applies: *a black dot relates to a strong relationship (9), a blank point is a medium relationship (3), a triangle encompasses a weak relationship (1), and an empty cell means that there is no interaction between customer's expectations and product specifications.* So is the *speed* with which the content of the suitcase can be found, strongly related to the *number of segments or compartments,* and to a lesser degree to the volume (weak relationship) and *opening angle* of the suitcase (medium relationship). *"Easy to carry"* has a strong relationship with the *volume* and a weak relationship with *"empty weight"* and *"material"* (see figure 3.27, part 5). Next, the project importance is indicated for each cell in a score.

$$Cell\ score = relationship's\ strength \times the\ weight\ (\%)$$

So, cell score *"easy to carry → volume"* = 9x 6 = 54.

Cell score *"easy to open → wear of the lock"* = 3 x 20 = 60, etc.

The sum of the cell scores per column indicates the priority of the technical parameters for the project. Accordingly, the technical parameter *"volume"* has a total score of 138 points and *"material"* has a total score of 150 points. All these scores are then added up. In this example it is 1616 points. Next, the priority per technical parameter is indicated, i.e. which product specifications deserve special attention in order to meet the demands of the customers? In this example, the parameters *"number of opening steps"*, *"number of segments"*, and *"lock wear"* have the highest priority of 21 %, 19 % and 14 % respectively. In the redesigning phase, these specifications received special attention.

Step 6: Interactions between product specifications (technical parameters).

The interactions between the technical parameters are indicated in the roof of the House of Quality. The *"number of segments"* has a weak relationship with *"empty weight"* and a medium relationship with *"volume"*. *"Lock wear"* has a strong relationship with *"closing force"* and a medium relationship with *"number of opening steps"* and *"safety lock"*. All these relationships are made explicit in the roof of the House of Quality, which is important for improvement of product specifications.

Step 7: Technical analysis

In this part of the House of Quality (part 7 in figure 3.27) the measure unit of all technical parameters is indicated (HOW MANY). For example, the measure unit of *"volume"* is cm^3, the measure unit of *"closing force"* is Newton (N) and the measure unit of *"empty weight"* is kg. Next, our product and the competitive product are technically evaluated on these parameters. Our case has 6 steps to open it, whereas the competitive product requires four. Our lock is also lasting till 5000 acts of use, whereas the lock of the competitive product starts showing defects after 3500 acts of use.

Step 8: Target value

Target values are determined based on the technical data and the priorities of the parameters. Target values regard the improvements of technical parameters which management pursues. Design teams executed these improvements. In this example, the emphases were mainly on reducing the number of steps to open the case, for which a target value of 2 is chosen. The solution to this problem was a central *safety lock* as locking principle. With this, the durability has been improved even further. Furthermore, the *number of segments* has also been increased (from 5 to 8) to improve the clarity of the arrangement.

3.2.15 Tree diagram

What is it?

A tree diagram systematically breaks down a topic into its component elements, and shows the logical and sequential links between these elements.

When do you use it?

A tree diagram is used to show the relationships between a topic and its component elements.

How do you use it?

Steps for drafting a tree diagram (NEN-ISO, 9004-4,1993):

1. Clearly and simply state the topic to be studied.
2. Define the major categories of the topic. Brainstorm or use the header cards from the affinity diagram.
3. Construct the diagram by placing the topic in a box on the left-hand-side. Branch the major categories laterally to the right.
4. For each major category, define the component elements and any sub-elements.
5. Laterally branch the component elements and sub-elements for each major category to the right.
6. Review the diagram to ensure that there are no gaps in either sequence or logic.

Example

Figure 3.28 shows a tree diagram which represents a telephone answering machine.

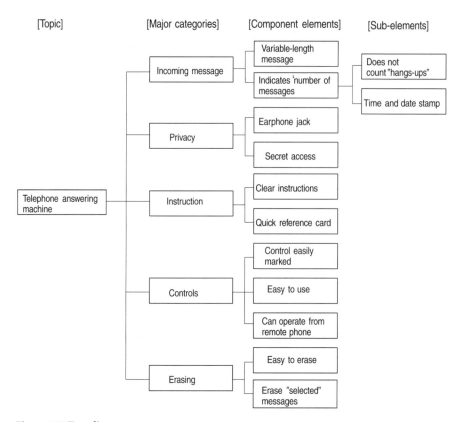

Figure 3.28 Tree diagram

Summarizing the tools and techniques

In table 3.9, a summarized view is given of the different tools and techniques in relation to their applicability per phase in the problem solving discipline.

Table 3.9. Overall view of tools & techniques

	Defining the problem	Analyzing root causes	Generating solutions	Planning and implementation	Measuring	Standardization
Brainstorming	●	●	●	●		
Affinity diagram	●	●	●			
Benchmarking	●	●	●			
Fishbone diagram	●	●	●	●		
Check sheet	●	●			●	
Flow chart	●	●		●	●	
Line graph	●	●			●	●
Run chart	●	●			●	●
Histogram	●	●			●	
Pareto-diagram	●	●	●			
Failure Mode and Effect Analysis	●	●	●	●		
Scatter diagram	●	●			●	
Control chart	●	●			●	●
Quality Function Deployment	●	●	●	●		
Tree diagram	●	●	●			

4 Interpersonal skills

The second pillar of the TQM-house encompasses interpersonal skills (see figure 4.1). This regards the skills required to support, guide, and stimulate quality behavior. The most important aspects of interpersonal skills that play a role in TQM are: *listening, questioning, building up on ideas of others, constructive arguing, clarifying, summarizing, involving others, showing appreciation,* and *giving feed back.* Application of these skills result in stronger customer orientation, effective teamwork, better performances through collective problem solving, and improved decision-making. Thus, without listening and verbal skills it is impossible to solve problems systematically, work effectively together, or achieve quality improvements. The more persons acquire these skills in the company, the better the effect will be on the business culture and activities. Good mutual communication between people is of essential importance here.

4.1 Communication

4.1.1 Knowledge

Communication is the exchange of messages between persons. It is the means by which people share ideas, clarify thinking and create a common understanding. The related communication goals regard influencing the factor knowledge. Knowledge can be looked upon as the personal ability of people, which is a function of information, culture and skills (Rampersad, 1998):

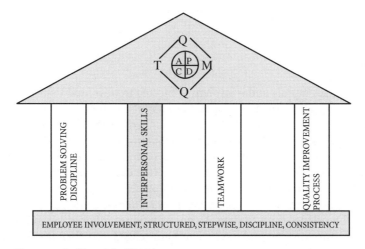

Figure 4.1 The second pillar of the TQM-house

$$\boxed{\text{<Knowledge>}=f(\text{<Information>}, \text{<Culture>}, \text{>Skills>})}$$

The function f specifies the relationship between knowledge on one side, and information, culture and skills on the other. Information comprises the meaning attributed to data obtained according to certain conventions, also known as *explicit* knowledge (Weggeman, 1997). Complete information is the basis for problem solving. Culture on the other hand, is the summary of norms, values, concepts, principles and attitudes of people, which underlie their behavior and their functioning. Skills are related to the competence, ability, capability, and personal experience of people. The knowledge components culture and skills represent *implicit* knowledge, which depends on the individual. This is difficult to describe, based on experience, practical in nature and finds its source, among other things, in associations, intuitions and fantasies. Explicit knowledge on the other hand, does not depend on the individual. It is theoretical in nature and specific in the form of procedures, theories, equations, manuals, drawings, etc. Physical labor, capital, and raw materials are, to an increasing extent, pushed aside by the factor knowledge (Drucker, 1985, 1993). Knowledge has now become the most important source for competitive advantage. Companies are therefore increasingly being transformed into *intelligent enterprises* and *e-businesses*, in which knowledge is being produced, absorbed and adequately commercialized. Companies which possess more knowledge than their competitors and which have the capability to develop a customer-oriented mentality and to convert knowledge into added value, are more profitable.

> *The wealth of nations is increasingly based on the creation and exploitation of knowledge. The best possible advantage must be taken of this new form of progress available to Community firms since it is an area in which the Community enjoys a substantial lead.*
>
> ICIMS NEWS

4.1.2 Learning

Knowledge ages rapidly and is strongly subjected to wear, and that is why people must continuously learn. Learning is a process of continuous knowledge enrichment or actualization of knowledge. Permanent education of workers at all levels within the organization, *in teamwork, communicative/social skills, quality improvement, and leadership skills among others are essential to realize* competitive advantage. This improves the employability (the capacity to remain employed), which offers a good guaranty against unemployment. Employees must, in view of the increasing shift from *lifetime employment to lifetime employability*, make sure that their knowledge is up-to-date. An organization is more successful when their employees learn quicker and implement knowledge faster than the competitors. An organization that does not learn continuously and is not able to continuously

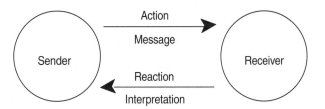

Figure 4.2 Communication model

register, develop, share, mobilize, cultivate, implement, evaluate, and spread knowledge cannot compete effectively. The ability of an organization to improve existing skills and to learn new ones is the most solid competitive advantage (Hamel & Prahalad, 1994). Therefore, it is necessary to continuously know which knowledge is essential, where this is available within the organization, which employee is equipped with it, how this knowledge can be adequately utilized, how this can be shared with others, how this knowledge will lead to added value, and how it can be maintained. The physical knowledge infrastructure within the organization must be organized in such a way that creativity, positive thinking, and self esteem are stimulated; for example, teamwork, use of computers, Internet and Intranet, establishment of a knowledge-bank, presence of a library, continuous training, etc. Furthermore, it can be stated that the ability of an organization to learn from experience depends on the willingness of the employees to reflect upon problems, the opportunity which is given to employees to identify and solve common problems as a team, the willingness to intervene preventively, and a working climate whereby every employee feels responsible for the company's performance. In practice, organizations only learn if employees have a sense of direction through a common and ambitious collective ambition (mission and vision), and work with all their ability to realize this ambition. Consequently, employees feel a strong bond with each other and are motivated to learn collectively (see chapter 9). Under these inspiring circumstances, they are also willing to share their knowledge with their colleagues and attune their personal goals with the organizational goals. And so, learning or vision driven organizations emerge in which learning is collective and based on a common collective ambition.

> *Quality is about learning. Quality is about being curious – it's about wanting to find out. It's the opposite of complacency, and it requires a lot of teaching, a lot of coaching, a lot of discussions with people. The learning process never stops. Don't think you can devise a nice programme or delegate it to somebody else and think quality has been taken care of.*
>
> Jan D. Timmer, former President Philips Electronics

4.1.3 Communication process

Communication is intended to enhance knowledge components by:

1. The exchange of information, informing people and the creation of clearness, in order to make the right decisions.
2. The creation of awareness for norms and values in the organization. Influencing opinions or attitudes of the people and cultivating the concept of cultural change and continuous improvement.
3. The development of skills such as the ability to listen well, to set priorities, to plan activities, etc.

Realization of these communication goals requires control of the communicative process. This process encompasses a sender who transmits a message to a receiver, who interprets the message and sends a reaction to the sender. This feedback enables the sender to verify whether the message was received and understood. Communication is thus a continuous cycle of action and reaction, see figure 4.2.

When people communicate with each other, they act as sender and receiver of messages. Communication is only successful if the receiver interprets the message, which was intended by the sender. The sender and receiver can disturb this communication process due to their different mental capacities. This is created by, among other things, upbringing, environments, education, experience, norms and values.

Mutual communication between people includes talking and writing. Talking can include the following aspects:

1. *Spoken language (verbal)*. The use of words, such as use of long complex or short easy sentences, which language someone speaks, if he speaks in the "I" or "we" form, etc. From this, the level of education and intelligence can be determined.
2. *Sound variations*. This regards sounds that do not belong to the spoken language, such as volume, accent, clearness, speaking velocity, laughing, crying, "eh", and "mm". From this, the feelings of people can be deduced. So is nervousness identified with high speech velocity and a quivering voice.
3. *Visible information (non-verbal)*. This includes everything except sound. Thus, attitude, head movements, eye contact, facial expressions, motions, clothes, yes-nodding, hand signals, blushing out of shyness, turning pale out of fear, scratching, playing with objects during lengthy stories, etc.

Non-verbal communication is distinguishable in five categories:

1. *Posture.* Shoulders hanging to the front (weak, sense of inferiority), head up (self-assured, proud), crossed legs (sure), feet under the chair (suspicion), etc
2. *Mimic. R*egards all facial expressions, such as wide opened eyes (amazed, startled), blinking (nervous), looking straight in the eyes (interested), avoiding

eye contact (insecure), firmly closed mouth (determined), blushing (shyness, excitement), turning pale (fright, fear, rage), etc.
3. *Signs.* Hand in the sides (superior), hands on the back (pensive, passive), closed fist (angry, excited), hand on the mouth (shy, insecure), head resting in the hands (pensive), movement with the index finger (drawing attention to), arranging ones spectacles (hesitating), cleaning spectacles (saving time), etc.
4. *Distance.* The real distance between people while communicating. Most contact with others takes place at approximately an arms length. Strangers usually keep a greater distance, while people who know each other well usually stand at half an arm's length.
5. *The use of voice.* Such as loudness, articulation, speaking rhythm, and speaking breaks.

Table 4.1 shows how a negative nonverbal message can produce negative reactions.

Table 4.1 Common nonverbal cues that produce negative reactions (G. Michael Barton, 1990)

Nonverbal Cue	Signal Received	Reaction From Reciever
Manager looks away when talking to the employee	I do not have this person's undivided attention	My supervisor is too busy to listen to my problem or simply does not care
Failure to acknowledge greeting from fellow employee	This person is unfriendly	This person is unapproachable
Ominous glaring (i.e., the evil eye)	I am angry	Reciprocal anger, fear, or avoidance depending on who is sending the signal in the organization
Rolling of the eyes	I am not being taken seriously	This person thinks he or she is smarter or better than I am
Deep sighing	Disgust or displeasure	My opinions do not count. I must be stupid or boring to this person
Heavy breathing (sometimes accompanied by hand waving)	Anger or heavy stress	Avoid this person at all costs
Eye contact not maintained when communicating	Suspicion and/or uncertainty	What does this person have to hide?
Manager crosses arms and leans away	Apathy and closed-mindedness	This person already has made up his or her mind; my opinions are not important
Manager peers over glasses	Skepticism or distrust	He or she does not believe what I am saying
Continues to read a report when employee is speaking	Lack of interest	My opinions are not important enough to get the supervisor's undivided attention

The comprehensibility of the message from the sender can be improved by:

- *simplicity of style;* comprehensible formulation, easy words, short sentences.
- *a recognizable structure*; a clear argument, whereby people know where they are heading.
- *conciseness;* stick to the essentials (brief).
- *a stimulating style;* such as frankness, asking questions, regard the other as adequate and as equal.

Communication involves asking the right questions, listening to the answers you get, and reacting to these answers. To achieve effective communication, the receiver should listen intensively, for instance by: asking open questions, summarizing, explaining, and being alert.

Good mutual communication is not only necessary while being in contact with external customers, but also while being in contact with employees. It is the duty of the manager to create a working environment in which effective communication can be developed. This can be done with the following methods:

- be honest and open and give everyone the necessary information, horizontally as well as vertically, and top-down as well as bottom-up;
- speak about *we* and not about *you* and *I;*
- don't ignore your employees;
- inform about the opinions and views of your employees;
- explain in advance why certain measures will be taken;
- listen attentively and give constructive feedback;
- place yourself in the other person's position;
- understand people and meet them halfway;
- avoid ego-remarks such as "*my years of experience shows that…*", *I know what I'm talking about*", etc.;
- emphasize the objectives;
- develop and create awareness for a common, ambitious, and inspiring mission and vision (see chapter 9);
- don't look for a scapegoat.

4.2 Interpersonal communication

The most important elements of interpersonal communication which play a role in TQM can be divided in: *listening, questioning, building up on ideas of others, constructive arguing, clarifying, summarizing, involvement, showing appreciation and giving feedback* (Reik, 1972; Pareek & Rao, 1990; PA Consulting Group, 1991). These skills will be briefly described in this paragraph and according to the following parts: *What is it? How do you use it? and Example(s).*

4.2.1 Listening

What is it?

Communication starts with good listening but there is a difference between listening and hearing. When someone listens, the words are actively registered and processed in the brain and then used. On the other hand, when someone hears, the words are registered in the brain and then nothing is done with it. Listening can thus be seen as, hearing, understanding, remembering and using it. Table 4.2 displays the difference between good and bad listening.

Table 4.2 Good listeners vs. bad listeners

Good listeners	Bad listeners
Are quiet when the other is expressing his opinions and tries to understand what is meant.	Interrupts the other before he is finished
Non-verbal behavior such as nodding or looking straight at the person.	Non-verbal behavior such as playing with objects or wobbling.

Some other bad listening habits are (Thomas, 1995; Culligan, et. al., 1983):

- not paying attention, thinking of something else, playing with paper on the desk or interrupting the conversation by answering the phone;
- act as if you are listening;
- listen until you have something to say, stop listening and then braise yourself to interrupt the other person when the next opportunity occurs;
- emotional sensitivity and prejudice;
- hearing what you expect, thinking that you hear what you expected or refuse to hear what you don't want to hear;
- focused on points of disagreement, looking for a chance to attack, to listen intensive for something you don't agree with instead of concentrating on the positive aspects;
- being turned off by the other and therefore being disinterested;
- only listening to the facts;
- cutting off when something is boring and not interesting.

How do you use it?

Be quiet for a while when the other is expressing his opinion, because people usually come to the point at the end of their story. Some recommendations for effective listening are:

- listen critically and intensively to the whole message; listen for ideas, feelings, intentions and facts, and extract the most important themes.
- suspend your opinion; don't jump to conclusions before the other has finished speaking.

- don't be distracted by external disturbances and the way of presentation; concentrate on what is said, pay attention to the speaker and show that you are intensively listening by making eye contact with the other and through verbal and non-verbal means to show that you understand him.
- concentrate on the contents and not on the "packaging";
- wait before reacting; if you react too soon, you can listen less intensively and therefore assimilate insufficient information. Don't be tempted to interrupt at the first opportunity.
- be prepared to react on ideas, suggestions and remarks without denouncing them;
- don't concentrate on what you expect to hear; don't anticipate what the other is going to say and let the other finish talking;
- suppress your prejudices;
- suppress the need to react emotionally on what is said or on what you think is said;
- try to organize what you hear;
- take notes occasionally; don't be distracted by taking notes continuously.
- prepare yourself mentally to start listening.

In other words, listening requires openness, patience and the will to understand others.

Technique for listening

Listen till the end, until the other has finished speaking and then give an answer. Try to place yourself in the other's position, in order to understand the situation better. Show the other that you take him/her seriously and that you are making an effort to understand him/her.

Examples of remarks to show that you are really listening

- From your words I understand that you don't agree with ………. *Is that correct?*
- *As I listen to you, it seems that you are very disappointed about* …………

4.2.2 Questioning

What is it?

Questioning gives you the opportunity to receive actual information from the other, or to know what someone's opinion is about a certain subject. Two types of questions can be distinguished: *open and closed questions. Open questions* are meant to invite someone to give elaborate information about opinions and feelings. They are usually also used to involve people in a conversation. Open questions usually start with the words *what, when, why, who, which, where,* or *how.*

Open questions invite and stimulate participation and involvement. By asking an open question, all possibilities for answering this question are left open, which can result in broadening and deepening the contact. These questions are meant to ask for a clarification, and to stimulate discovery. *Closed questions* are used to place the emphasis on something or to get a yes or no answer. You can guide the conversation this way. These questions can be used to quickly obtain direct information. Unfortunately, they are less useful because the answer on these questions is usually yes or no. To obtain a complete picture, it is important to ask open questions.

Open and closed questions can be subdivided in the following types of questions:

- informative questions; questions for actual information.
- direct questions; these questions lead the person to think in a certain direction. This limits the answer possibilities and limited information is obtained.
- multiple choice questions; questions with alternatives.
- suggestive questions; the answer is already included in these questions, which is based on the expectation and perception of the questioner.
- chain questions; a question composed of several questions.
- opinion questions; to ask the opinion of the other.

How do you use it?

Ask as many open questions as possible with the purpose to increase involvement, prevent indistinctness, reveal precious information and ideas, and correct out dated views. The results of questioning are for instance: more focused discussions, better-supported decisions and evidence of respect and interest. Questions to be avoided when coaching teams are (Pareek & Rao, 1990):

- critical and sarcastic questions; to rebuke the other or to call in question his/her ability, whereby a gap is developed between leader and employees. These questions can lead to grudge, hostility and the suppression of ideas. Example:" why didn't you finish the assignment within the deadline?" contains criticism, were as "how can you explain that you're late for the deadline?" is an invitation to search for the causes.
- annoying questions; are meant to check if the other is right or wrong (type of interrogation); implicate a superior attitude of the leader.
- suggestive questions. These questions put the wrong answers in the employee's mouth. For instance:" couldn't you meet the deadline because of other problems within the company?". This leads to answers the leader wants to hear and consequently, blocks a closer examination of the problem.

Technique for questioning
Ask the right type of question (preferably open questions). Question in such a way that the other gets more space and feels more involved in the conversation.

Examples

Open question: *what do you mean by that? what do you mean? how does that work? what do you think about that? when will that happen? who will execute that process? etc.*

Closed question: *did you or did you not receive the book? is the working environment in our organization good or bad? would you like a green or a blue one?*

Informative question: *since when have you been working there?*

Direct question: *do you prefer David or John as chief?*

Suggestive question: *is it also your opinion that...., don't you also think that..., you approve of the working environment, don't you?*

Chain question: *how do you execute the process? and did you approach Frank about this? what is his opinion?*

Opinion question: *do you find this work meaningful?*

4.2.3 Building up on ideas of others

What is it?

People continuously generate ideas. It is important that you are able to build up on ideas of others, which results in more and better ideas. This implies that you adopt someone's suggestion and add something of your own to it.

How do you use it?

Give credit to the idea of someone else and then suggest improvements and supplements. This way, fewer ideas are lost and better-considered solutions are obtained. This also leads to a feeling of appreciation for the person who gave the idea. Building up on someone's ideas is intended to elaborate, improve and convert someone's idea into successful actions. It is therefore important to always take ideas seriously. A reward within the company for the best idea can produce useful suggestions.

Technique for building up on ideas of others
Express your appreciation for the idea of the other and then add something of yourself to it.

Examples

Yes, because then we have ....
A good idea, Howard. This gives us the opportunity to ....

4.2.4 Constructive arguing

What is it?

Make differences in opinion known in a positive and constructive way, to make a constructive contribution to a discussion. The conversation is thus broadened whereby new ideas and opinions can be developed.

How do you use it?

Make objections known in a positive and constructive manner. State another view or motivate why according to your opinion, the idea should not be accepted. Correct inaccurate statements and offer other views. By doing so, you will obtain more clearness, better involvement, and better decision-making.

> **Techniques for constructive arguing**
> Analyze the idea of the other and give an alternative opinion. State reasons why according to you, the idea should not be accepted.

Examples

That can be true, but look at it from the point of view of......
I don't think it is a good idea, because it is coupled with.....

4.2.5 Clarifying

What is it?

Interpret and repeat clearly and distinctly in your own words what the other has said. Experience indicates that in approximately 50 % of all cases misunderstandings occur if the statement of the other is not clarified.

How do you use it?

Ask a question to be certain that you understood the intention of the other. Thus, interpret what the other has said and repeat this in your own words and check if it is correct. Therefore you'll get fewer misunderstandings, more clearness, more objective discussions and a better understanding of personal feelings.

> **Techniques for clarifying**
> Interpret what the other has said and check if it is correct. Repeat the words of the other in your interpretation.

Examples

For all clearness, you say that.....
If I understand it clearly, it means that.......

4.2.6 Summarizing

What is it?

To summarize what is said and to repeat what is agreed upon and decided, you create clearness and structure in the discussion. Clarifying regards a point in the discussion, whereas a summary includes the entire previous conversation.

How do you use it?

Summarize at the beginning of a meeting the most important points of the previous meeting. Also give a summary before going to the next item on the agenda.

Techniques for summarizing

Repeat the most important decisions and agreements of a previous meeting.

Example

"Ok, let us start. During the previous meeting, we discussed a couple of possible solutions and eliminated a few so that eventually three solutions remained. Mr. Johnson was going to study the feasibility of the remaining solutions. Mr. Johnson, can you please give us the results?"

4.2.7 Involving others

What is it?

Involve the participants in a discussion in such a way that their active participation is stimulated.

How do you use it?

See to it that no one is excluded from the discussion. People who are silent for a period of time must be activated by asking them a question. And so, active participation is stimulated and also creates a feeling of self-esteem and strong motivation.

Techniques for involving others

Address the concerned individuals by name and ask a question to involve him/her in the discussion.

Examples

"Wilson, we have not heard you yet. What do you think of this solution?"
"Brown, you're out of the spotlight. What is your opinion about this?"

4.2.8 Showing appreciation

What is it?

Showing appreciation during a discussion in such a way to stimulate improved performance, stronger motivation and a feeling of self-esteem.

How do you use it?

One method to encourage employees to improve performance, is by expressing your appreciation every time someone strives and gets results. Indicate clearly what you're showing your appreciation for and for whom it is meant. Do this when others are present and shortly after the delivered performance. Appreciation can be a word of thanks or a compliment for something that someone has done or said correctly. The objective of this is to show that you've noticed someone's efforts, to stimulate people to deliver the same effort again, and to encourage others to deliver similar efforts.

Technique for showing appreciation

Express your appreciation for good performances immediately and clearly. Preferably, do this in the presence of others and make clear for whom it is meant.

Examples

"Very good, Diana. That was an excellent speech, thanks a lot".
"Finally, I would like to thank Kevin for all the work he has done ".

4.2.9 Giving feedback

What is it?

Feedback is a form of communication whereby the receiver of the message lets the sender know how the message comes across. As a result, one will know the effect his/her behavior has on the other. Annoying behavior can be corrected and shaped to the required behavior. Cooperation within the group becomes more open and effective.

How do you use it?

There are rules for the sender as well as for the receiver. The most important rules for the giver of feedback are:

- make clear to yourself beforehand what you want to say and collect the necessary data;
- start with positive points;

- make clear which effects the behavior of someone has on you; e.g. "The remark you just made irritated me, because I felt that I didn't do my utmost to solve the problem adequately".
- state your observation of the behavior of the other in the descriptive style (what you see) and not in the criticizing style; thus: "During the meeting you were not very talkative, why?" and not "Your participation in the meeting was bad, were you not interested?".
- focus on the behavior and not on the person; thus; "The remark you just made irritated me"; and not "You're someone who always wants to stand at the center with your funny remarks".
- refer to events that occur at that moment or have occurred recently; thus: "Your absence today is very annoying" and not: "In previous years you were also always absent".
- give the other the possibility to react; thus, listen intently and keep an open mind for the opinion of the other.
- show that you trust the other and end with positive remarks about the future.

The most important rules for the receiver of feedback are:

- listen attentively and closely before you accept the feedback, ask to clarify when it is not clear;
- don't go into defense or start attacking and don't look for explanations;
- accept the feedback and analyze why you're acting that way;
- consider that the giver of feedback is kindly disposed towards you; don't feel that you're being attacked.
- don't express negative feelings; study the feedback together with the giver.
- don't try to be humorous or smart; concentrate on a change for the better.

Technique for giving feedback
Decide for yourself if you'll give feedback or not and what you or the other will gain from it. If you'll give or receive feedback, use the previously mentioned rules.

Summarizing the interpersonal skills

A summarized review of all mentioned interpersonal skills is given in table 4.3.

Table 4.3 Summarized review of interpersonal skills

Listening		
Goal	*Result*	*Technique*
Gather information	Better understanding and being informed	Listen until the other has finished speaking, then reply. Try to imagine yourself in the other's situation, in order to understand the subject of discussion better. Show the other that he's taken seriously and you're making an effort to understand him.
Questioning		
Goal	*Result*	*Technique*
Obtain valuable information and ideas, increase involvement.	Better decisions and focussed discussions.	Ask the right type of question. Ask the questions in such a way that the other feels comfortable and involved in the discussion.
Building up on ideas of others		
Goal	*Result*	*Technique*
Developing and shaping of ideas.	More and better thought-out solutions and a feeling of appreciation.	Express your appreciation for the idea of the other and then add something of your own.
Constructive arguing		
Goal	*Result*	*Technique*
State other views and correct wrong statements.	Clearness, better decision making and involvement.	Analyze the other's idea and give an alternative view. Furnish reasons why the idea cannot be accepted.
Clarifying		
Goal	*Result*	*Technique*
To be certain that you've interpreted correctly what the other said.	More clearness, less misunderstandings and better listening skills	Interpret what the other has said and check if it is correct. Repeat the words of the other in according to your understanding.
Summarizing		
Goal	*Result*	*Technique*
Create insight in the most important points from the previous discussion.	Clearness and structure in a discussion.	Repeat the most important decisions and agreements from a previous meeting.

Table 4.3 (Continued)

Involving others		
Goal	*Result*	*Technique*
Stimulate better involvement and active participation	Create better listening skills, as well as self-esteem and stronger motivation	Address the respective person by name and ask a question to involve him/her in the meeting.
Showing appreciation		
Goal	*Result*	*Technique*
Stimulate to deliver the same effort again and urge others to do the same	Motivation and self-esteem	Show your appreciation for good performance immediately and clearly, preferably in the presence of others and state clearly whom it is meant for.
Giving feedback		
Goal	*Result*	*Technique*
Correct annoying behavior and shape it to get the required behavior. Cooperation in the group becomes more open and effective	More effective cooperation and open communication.	Decide for yourself if you will give the feedback or not and what you or the other will gain from it. If you will give and receive feedback, use the mentioned rules.

5 Teamwork

TQM is based on firm mutual collaboration between people, i.e. effective team-work. The third pillar of the TQM house relates to this aspect (see figure 5.1). Teamwork is the engine of TQM. Everything regarding TQM is done as a team. For successful teamwork, it is necessary that the team composition, the work climate, the style of meetings, the team members, and the leader comply with certain conditions. These aspects will be described in this chapter.

5.1 Team composition

A team consists of a group of people with complementary skills, who have a feeling of commitment to a common goal, who are charged with the execution of decisions taken, and whose work is influenced by these factors. It is not wise to put too many persons in a team, because this can work the wrong way. To guarantee effectiveness, the team should consist of 5 to 8 members and should have never more than 12 members. The team should also have different kinds of personalities. To increase the chance of success, it is recommended to establish cross-functional teams consisting of members from all affected groups. The teams must have the right composition. A balanced division of directly involved persons from different disciplines with different personal qualities is hereby necessary, as well as a leader with shared leadership roles.

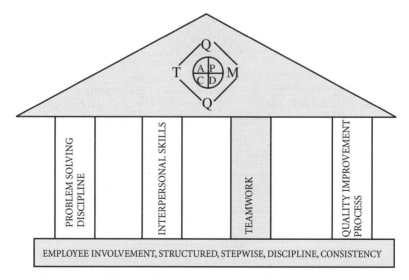

Figure 5.1 The third pillar of the TQM-house

An effective team is composed of members with a combination of several different qualities (see figure 5.2). These qualities should be evenly divided among all team members. In practice, a harmonious combination of six qualities are needed in a team (Groote, et al., 1995):

1. The **inspirer.** Is an innovator, has future vision and imagination, is goal oriented, develops new ideas, inspires others to seek challenges, and knows how to inspire and challenge people.
2. The **custodian.** At set times forces the team to mark time, creates order, resists change, is rigid and conservative, and integrates previous experiences in the work.
3. The **thinker.** Likes to analyze situations and lay connections, thinks clearly, logically and in an abstract manner, is detached, and cannot excite others.
4. The **practical person.** Is a doer, concrete, and interested in finding practical solutions, tests proposals with own experiences, likes lively meetings, and quits when others become too theoretical.
5. The **entrepreneur.** Takes initiatives, lead the way in everything that should be done, decided or said. The whole team is swept along by his enthusiasm and active way, is intolerant, puts others under great pressure, is a nag, and tries to do everything on his own.
6. The **supporter.** Shows good will, gives a friendly word on time, asks helpful questions, mediates, listens, never walks in front, and creates conditions for good results.

The qualities that stand opposite of each other in figure 5.2 do not exclude each other but are complementary.

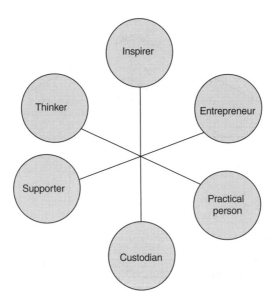

Figure 5.2 Six qualities

Question list regarding the six qualities

With the following question list, team members can determine which qualities they have more and which less and consequently, they can continuously control the quality of the team (Groote, et.al., 1995). The question list includes an aid mechanism with which a determination can be made as to which qualities each team member contributes most to a group. Based on the obtained insight in the distribution of the available qualities, measures can be taken to lessen the absence or abundant presence of certain qualities. Six half sentences are given in table 5.1, with six possibilities ("a" till "f"). If you recognize yourself completely in one of the possibilities, than award 10 points to this possibility. If you find more than one possibility suitable, than divide the 10 points according to your preference. Award most points to the possibility that best suits your behavior and conception. For example, in table 5.1, the score of question 1 is divided over a=4, b=3, c=1, and e=2.

Table 5.1 Question list of six qualities

No.	Score	possibilities	Half sentences
1			**I like my work, because I:**
	4	a	Like to analyze situations and look for the best solutions.
	3	b	Am interested in finding practical solutions; things that really work.
	1	c	Like to have the feeling that I develop good cooperative relationships.
		d	Can devote myself completely to my work and I feel comfortable.
	2	e	Like to find areas that trigger my imagination.
		f	Enjoy organizing (even what others do).
2			**Typically, when I work in a group I:**
		a	Make an effort to get better acquainted with my colleagues and to see to it that all my colleagues can have their say.
		b	Frequently think clearly about things, lay connections and I refute illogical arguments.
		c	Make an effort to continuously offer new suggestions that are tested to practical situations and to carry out the plans of the group.
		d	Always stay focused on what must be reached and I formulate the objectives based on my vision of the future. I am also capable of coming up with unexpected things.
		e	Continuously strive for perfection while executing each group activity.
		f	Determine what must be done if a decision must be made without much hesitation.

Table 5.1 (Continued)

3			Once I'm part of a team:
		a	I manage to guide people in a direction.
		b	It is my presence of mind that prevents us from overlooking matters or doing double work.
		c	I'm always willing to support and encourage others.
		d	I'm always seeking new ideas and developments.
		e	My judgement ability contributes to arriving at the right decisions.
		f	They can count on me to see to it that all important matters are carried out.
4			My most important contribution to a team is that I:
		a	Frequently discover new possibilities.
		b	Know how to manage a wide range of people.
		c	Can easily distance myself from daily details and objectively consider the situation.
		d	Work efficiently and make sure that others also work efficiently.
		e	Am willing to be unpopular (for a while) if that will lead to results.
		f	Because of my experience, usually know what is feasible and realistic.
5			A short coming I have when working in a team is perhaps that:
		a	I only feel at ease if meetings are structured and ordered; if it becomes vague or disorderly, I'll leave.
		b	I have the tendency to talk too much when I am involved in the discussion and I get new ideas.
		c	My critical attitude makes it difficult for me to follow the opinions and ideas of others eagerly and enthusiastically.
		d	I find it difficult to take the lead from the start (to take initiatives). Maybe because I'm very sensitive to a good atmosphere in the group.
		e	I have the tendency to be completely absorbed by ideas and ambitions that cross my mind, and therefore become impatient if others cannot keep up with me.
		f	I worry needlessly about details and matters that can go wrong.
6			A problem I face when I work in a group is that:
		a	I am impatient with those that stand in the way of improvement.
		b	My concern to do things well and well-considered can sometimes be an obstacle.
		c	I sometimes have to be stimulated by others to be concerned with matters that are being carried out.
		d	I sometimes don't understand why the results of my work are not accepted by others.
		e	I get irritated by the disorderly way others proceed.
		f	I sometimes seek support and confidence from others too quickly and therefore get disappointed in them and myself.

Now fill in your score in table 5.2, by marking your score for each question, behind the respective letters (in column S). You determine the total score per quality, by adding up the scores (behind the letters) horizontally (per quality) and registering this total score in the last column "total score". In table 5.2, the scores of question one (see table 5.1) are completed as an example. The total score indicates the qualities you contribute to the group.

Table 5.2 Score table

Type of quality	Question												Total score
	1		2		3		4		5		6		
		S		S		S		S		S		S	
Inspirer	e	2	d		d		a		e		a		
Thinker	a	4	b		e		c		c		c		
Entrepreneur	d		f		a		e		b		e		
Supporter	c	1	a		c		b		d		f		
Practical person	b	3	c		f		f		a		d		
Custodian	f		e		b		d		f		b		
S = Score per question				Total score add up horizontally------------->									

5.2 Team performance and team development

Important aspects when building up team performances are:

- Create urgency, make high demands on performance norms.
- Choose team members based on their skills and not on their personalities.
- Give extra attention to the first meetings and actions.
- Give clear rules of conduct.
- Give the team authority and ownership over processes for which they are responsible.
- Confront the group regularly with new facts and information.
- Spend a lot of time with each other.
- Use the power of feedback, appreciation, acknowledgement and intrinsic reward.
- Attempt a number of result-oriented tasks which can be carried out at once (as an example).

The development of a newly formed team can be distinguished into five phases (see figure 5.3):

1. **Formation.** In this phase, the team members learn to know each other, test the authority of the leader, see which way things go, are hesitant and unsure, observe the behavior of their colleagues, try to figure out what their place is within the team and try to work themselves up. Due to defensive and sometimes hostile behavior, there is little or no improvement. In this phase, there is a lot of talk without people understanding each other. In this phase, the team leader must help the group perform tasks and gain knowledge.

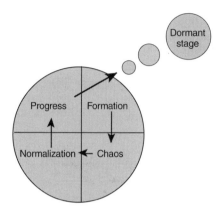

Figure 5.3 How teams develop themselves

2. **Chaos.** In this phase, the team members are aware of the long road ahead before the goals are reached, which is coupled with feelings of dissatisfaction, resistance, and frustration. There is also a tendency towards negative behavior, internal competition for attention and power, conflicts between group members and management, distrust of each other, emotional reactions to the tasks to be carried out and doubts about the usefulness of them. In this phase, the team leader must take serious notice of the feelings of discontent in the group, should avoid taking them personally and should discuss them without defensive behavior.
3. **Normalization.** Now the atmosphere is less tense. Cooperation and communication are improved. The members are getting used to each other, trust, accept and respect each other, whereby a team spirit is gradually formed and a sense of unity in the group develops. Now, there are constructive discussions. There is also more time spent on work and less on conflicts among themselves, which has a positive effect on the team performances. In this phase, the team leader must by all means concentrate on support and valuation of everyone's effort, improvement of the working atmosphere, mutual communication and cooperation.
4. **Progress.** There is now a creative working atmosphere, a strong related unity, good mutual communication and hard work to carry out the tasks. The team members know each other's strong and weak points and feel involved, whereby a lot of progress is made. Moreover, there is a continuous search for possibilities to improve mutual cooperation.
5. **Dormant stage.** The team members become easy-going, are confident with the success of the team's working procedures and mainly concentrate on maintaining stability of the team. In this phase, the team must view itself critically and adjust to the changed situation.

Remmerswaal (1992) identified three phases in the development of groups: the *starting group*, the *advanced group,* and the *mature group*. Table 5.3 shows a checklist which indicates the behavior these groups exhibit in the different phases of their development (Hoevenaars, et al., 1995). This behavior is related to the following dimensions: *result oriented, involvement & loyalty, improvement & renewing ability, customer-supplier thinking, communication, cooperation, conflict handling, guiding & coaching,* and *manners*. The phase in which the group is currently, can be determined with the checklist and also what should still be done to be able to work as a full-grown group (as a team). For example, the present profile of a group is given in table 5.3. This shows that for most of the dimensions, this group has not yet reached the mature phase.

Table 5.3 The development stages of a group

	Dimension	Starting group	Advanced group	Mature group
Accent on care for production	Result oriented	An individual is well-informed about the goals and performances of the group, and knows how to measure and improve performances.	Few know the goals and performances of the group, and know how to measure and improve the performances.	Every group member is well-informed about goals and performances of the group and knows how to measure and improve the performances.
	Involvement & loyalty	Group members are hardly interested in how the company functions now or in the future and don't do more than what is expected of them.	Group members read the information that is sent to them and occasionally ask management a question about it. Sometimes they are willing to do something extra but for appropriate compensation.	Group members are well-informed about their organization, now and in the future, help and think actively, and care about their work.
	Improvement & renewing ability	The group is not interested in improvement/renewal, doesn't offer ideas, and is not open to suggestions of others.	Sometimes they come up with an improvement proposal (through the suggestion box), assume an attitude of expectation, blame others for their failures.	The group offers ideas and suggestions for improvements or renewal of equipment, working method and or products, are involved until it is realized.
	Customer-suppliers thinking	The group does not know its customers and suppliers, does not get or give information about complaints, does not feel responsible for mistakes, blames others for them.	The group knows the names of its clients through the indirect feedback of complaints, tries to avoid making the same mistakes again, and has a vague idea about the application fields of the customer. There is no contact with the suppliers, but they know what is wrong with what is supplied.	The group knows and visits its clients and suppliers, directly receives and gives signals about complaints and holds discussions about improvements, wishes, and demands. It feels responsible for the delivered quality.

Table 5.3 (Continued)

	Communication patterns	The group has no need for deliberations internally, or with others or to participate and help thinking, is hardly interested in how others handle matters, does not want feedback about its functioning.	The group meets on a regular basis because it is expected, does not really know what to discuss, does not take initiatives to include or inform others from outside the group, but cries out for "more participation", doubts feedback about its functioning, wants to learn from others when it is suitable.	The group takes its own initiatives to deliberate, involves the necessary persons/departments, wants to hear/learn from others how they handle certain matters, and wants feedback about its functioning.
Accent on care for people	*Cooperation*	The group fits as loose sand together. The members are not interested in each other and cannot replace each other. They work for themselves, do their own tasks. All responsibility is for the group leader. New co-workers have to learn the ropes by themselves.	They are somewhat aware of each other's characteristics and capacities and take it into consideration, can replace each other partially, try to increase the exchange capacity and try to train new colleagues for several activities.	The group has a strong bond, the members take each other into consideration, can replace one another and anticipate in each other's absence. New colleagues are welcomed and guided without any problems.
	Conflict handling	Opposing opinions and behavior in the group are not open to discussion, the discussions about this are being avoided, or otherwise there is a quarrel. Group members keep their points of view and do not give in.	Opposing opinions and behavior can sometimes be discussed, depending on the influence of the different team members. Some members usually get the worst of it and others seldom.	Opposing opinions and behaviors are open for discussion, are clearly discussed and lead to improvements. Individuals are willing to make concessions for the benefit of the group.
	Guiding & coaching	The group has a strong need for guidance on tasks and responsibilities. Management must carry through corrections. The group gives no signals about training needs, they only follow the necessary ones.	The group has regular doubts or disagreements and therefore a need for guidance by managers to take decisions. They go to all the training programs suggested by management but never come up with their own ideas.	The group has their own direction regarding tasks, responsibilities and behavior. They correct each other when necessary, indicate educational needs and are trained in a broad field.

Table 5.3 (Continued)

	Manners	How to behave is not open for discussion. Nothing is mentioned about rules and norms. There is no basis for trust; they do not dare to admit mistakes. They usually comment arrogantly about others. Their own interest prevails above that of the group.	There are a few common rules and norms in the group about certain matters, but not everything is discussible. Mutual trust grows, but certain mistakes are hidden out of fear for negative remarks. The vision, which combines own and group interests, is strengthened.	Manners and behavior are discussible. It is clear to everyone where he or she stands. There is a broad basis of trust, mistakes are reported spontaneously and discussed to learn from them. Group interest follows naturally from own interest.

5.3 Conducting effective meetings

Holding meetings is a mean of communication to give, receive and exchange information, solve problems, take initiatives and /or negotiate. A meeting encompasses a group of people who discuss an item which was scheduled beforehand, under supervision of a chairperson. It is hereby important that:

- The objectives of the meeting are clear.
- The right people attend the meeting. Invite only those that are indispensable.
- The meeting is evaluated with a focus on improvement possibilities (see table 5.6).
- A chairperson is appointed to lead the meeting, a minute taker to take the minutes, a timekeeper to check the time and a process keeper to guard the communication process; see to it that they listen to each other, don't speak in confusion, reach consensus, brainstorm in the correct way, etc.
- The meeting starts on time.
- The meeting is closed as soon as the objective of the meeting has been reached.
- A clear agenda is made; the items of the agenda are divided into discussion items (minimal 20 minutes per item), and information items (minimal 2 to 10 minutes per item); these two groups of items should be separated during the meeting.
- The agenda is put together beforehand and circulated, so everyone can prepare for the meeting.
- The agenda is not deviated from.

Example of an agenda
1. Opening
2. Announcements
3. Minutes from the previous meeting
4. Discussion and decision-making about...

5. Other issues to be discussed
6. Questions
7. Closing

Questions which are central when conducting a meeting are:

- What subject is it about?
- Who should attend and who should not?
- When and where will the meeting be held?
- What are the requirements for the meeting room?
- Should guest speakers be invited?
- Is the agenda made and sent to all the participants beforehand?
- Who is the timekeeper?
- Who is the process keeper?
- Who will take the minutes?

During discussion, an account of the meeting should take place. Therefore, someone who can listen well, writes fluently, and can quickly extract the essential details from a discussion, should be chosen to take the minutes. The objective of the minutes is to register agreements and to guarantee continuity. Important points in the minutes are:

- Which questions were discussed?
- Which answers were given?
- Which arguments and considerations were important?
- Which conclusions were drawn?
- Which decisions were taken?
- Which actions will be undertaken?
- Which agreements were made (who will do what and when)?
- Attendance registration.
- Date for the next meeting.

The minutes must include clear, brief and neatly arranged information about these items. Table 5.4 gives a review of the most important roles and tasks of the meeting.

Table 5.4 Tasks and roles of the meeting

Chairperson

Characteristics of the chairperson: knowledgeable, experienced, enthusiastic, decisive, and good communicative skills.

Prior to the meeting

1. Provide the right team composition.
2. Read the minutes of the previous meeting and formulate the agenda and objectives of the meeting.
3. Send invitations, agenda and additional information to the participants on time and provide an adequate meeting room.
4. Prepare yourself.

During the meeting

1. Ask if everyone has received the information and can be present during the entire meeting
2. Discuss reporting (who will take the minutes), the objectives of the meeting and the expected contribution of the participants.
3. Delegate supporting tasks to a timekeeper and a process keeper.
4. Go through the agenda according to the written order.
5. Guard the meeting process by: asking questions, summarizing opinions, asking silent persons for their opinions, clarifying opinions, stimulating listening, expressing appreciation, accentuating conclusions, etc.
6. Give a summary of the most important points and stimulate discussions focused on realizing the team goals.
7. Ask questions such as: who has a suggestion? who agrees and who is against? Who wants to comment on this? who can complete or clarify this? who has counter-arguments? who can summarize this?
8. Establish relationships between the different ideas and stimulate open communication.
9. Ask for facts, suggestions and information, and focus on what must be realized.
10. Do not tolerate late comers, private discussions and leaving.
11. Do not permit moving away from the subject and determine clearly who will do what.
12. Take stimulating actions to keep the meeting going if it threatens to come to a deadlock.
13. See to it that all available information is accessible to all participants.
14. Stay neutral with respect to the subject and the participants; threat everyone as an equal.
15. Do not discuss more than one agenda item at a time.
16. Maintain a relaxed, informal and disciplined atmosphere.
17. End the discussion as soon as the subject has been treated extensively.
18. Evaluate the effectiveness of the team.
19. Strive for one mindedness, since absolute consensus is not required.

Table 5.4 (Continued)

Participants

Prior to the meeting

1. Read the minutes of the previous meeting, study the agenda and prepare yourself.
2. Figure out what the objective of the meeting is, sympathize with it and stick to it.
3. Be on time.

During the meeting

1. Make sure that your items are on the agenda and stick to the agenda items that are being discussed.
2. If you do not understand certain statements, ask for clarification.
3. Participate actively by: listening well, summarizing opinions, asking for clarification, building up on ideas of others, making constructive arguments, not moving away from the subject, etc.
4. Say it if you have something to say and be silent if that is not the case.
5. Avoid remarks that will divide the team and make notes of the agreements.
6. Accept the chairperson.
7. Contribute to the solution and do not create more problems.
8. Don't be noisy, don't hinder progress and don't participate with a hidden agenda.
9. Do not be guided by emotions but remain objective.

After the meeting

1. Do what was agreed upon, do not complain about the decisions taken, and do not try to reverse decisions outside the meeting (discuss this in the following meeting).
2. Do not broadcast what was said during the meeting.

Timekeeper

1. Monitor how much time the team takes to execute its tasks.
2. Give directions about how to spend time.
3. Discuss the planned duration of each agenda item at the beginning of the meeting.
4. Interrupt the team when it exceeds the available time.
5. Give suggestions about possible adjustments of the agenda.
6. Continuously guard the pace at which the different phases of the meetings are reviewed.
7. The meeting should not be more than one hour and a half.

Process keeper

The process keeper is responsible for effective use of problem solving techniques, and the development of inter-personal skills of the team members.

1. Evaluations are not allowed during brainstorming sessions.
2. All participants must actively participate in the problem solving discussions.
3. The team should continuously strive for one-mindedness.
4. Problem solving techniques and tools must be used when necessary.
5. All activities should be walked through in phases.
6. Do they have an open mind for the opinions and suggestions of others?

Table 5.5 Elements of teamwork

Decisions to take	Decision-making process
– Formulate goals – Define all tasks – Budget time and resources	– Use the problem solving discipline and quality improvement process
Supportive activities	**Interpersonal skills**
– Keep the time (Timekeeper) – Take minutes (Minute taker) – Make notes on a flip-chart – Guard and evaluate the teamwork process (Process keeper) – Organize coffee, tea, and cold drinks – Book and arrange the meeting room. Look for an isolated location without a telephone, interruptions, or distractions. Tables and chairs must be arranged in a U-form. See to it that there is a flip-chart, overhead projector, blank transparency sheets, and markers. – Make agreements about smoking and breaks	– Listening – Questioning – Building up on ideas of others – Arguing constructively – Clarifying – Summarizing – Involving others – Showing appreciation – Giving feedback

Table 5.5 displays some important elements of teamwork that play a role in a meeting. Table 5.6 displays a form which can be used to evaluate the teamwork process. After the meeting, each team member must first answer the assertions in the table for himself (with a number 1 till 4), after which the scores will be discussed in the group. Indicate here what could be better.

Table 5.6 Teamwork evaluation form

Everyone listened till the end	1	2	3	4
Mostly open questions were asked	1	2	3	4
Other's ideas were build upon	1	2	3	4
The arguments were constructive	1	2	3	4
The remarks of others were clarified	1	2	3	4
Previous conversations were summarized	1	2	3	4
Silent persons were involved	1	2	3	4
Appreciation was expressed	1	2	3	4
Feedback was given	1	2	3	4
Relevant information was exchanged among team members	1	2	3	4
The opinions of team members were clearly expressed	1	2	3	4
We were in agreement and spoke the same language	1	2	3	4
There was no struggle for power among members	1	2	3	4
Everyone said what he/she thought about it; we felt free to express our opinions (there was an outspoken discussion)	1	2	3	4
There were no small intimate parties	1	2	3	4

Table 5.6 (Continued)

It was clear what we were working on and the discussions were purposeful	1	2	3	4
Everyone had to fulfil a clear task: Timekeeper – process keeper – minute taker – conduct keeper - gather information – give presentations - work out a time schedule	1	2	3	4
We followed a clear method	1	2	3	4
The team aimed at harmony and consensus	1	2	3	4
The team members had respect and trust in each other	1	2	3	4
Circle the correct number: 1 = never/no/it is not correct, 2 = once in a while/hardly, 3 = frequent/ usually well, 4 = always/yes/it is correct				

5.4 The role of the team members

For effective teamwork, it is important that team members stick to certain rules (also see table 5.4). Thus, all team members should:
- Devote themselves to the common team goals based on a common mission and vision.
- Feel themselves responsible and equal.
- Be interested and motivated.
- Accept, appreciate, and respect each other.
- Give high priority to continuous improvement.
- Participate actively with the activities of the team.
- Know, trust, help, understand, and complete each other.
- Know their clients.
- Communicate openly and have an open mind for the expectations of their surroundings.
- Make free use of and want to make use of each other's information.
- Have a positive attitude towards others, whereby the interest of the organization is more important than that of the department.
- Channel the experiences from the team back to their own working environment.
- Abide by the decisions taken by the team.
- Be responsible for their own contribution as well as for the results of the team.
- See problems as a means for improvements; welcome problems as opportunities.
- Be aware of and recognize their responsibility for improvement.
- Make personal improvement a routine.
- Be good listeners.
- Recognize the processes they own.
- Use a systematic approach to improvement.

5.5 The role of the leader

Effective teamwork requires effective leadership. The leader should:

- Set clear goals and provide challenging tasks.
- Demonstrate constantly through his own actions and words that he is never satisfied with anything less than continuous improvement.
- State clearly when something should be finished.
- Place himself in the position of the employees.
- Not evade or obscure problems of the team.
- Listen actively to employees and express appreciation for their improvements.
- Let employees keep their self-esteem and respect and stimulate their qualities; stimulate them to perform to the best of their ability.
- Help employees accept responsibility and think for themselves.
- Create a basis of trust, respect and open communication; be honest and predictable and develop a position of trust. Employees who trust their leaders and who are trusted and respected in turn, will share their knowledge with management. This is the most important way to ensure individual participation and continuous improvement.
- Give the other the acknowledgement which is due.
- Show employees that he is committed to improvement efforts and that he has recognized their achievements.
- Stimulate employees to be involved.
- Convince employees that the chosen path is the correct one.
- Teach employees to realize that the company's interest and their interest are geared into one another.
- Help employees separate essentials from side issues.
- Make employees conscious of their strong points and shortcomings, in order to let them function more effectively.
- Be interested in the development of his employees.
- Look for someone's potential possibilities.
- Uphold high norms and values, and let it be known.
- Promote a learning process.
- Adjust his pattern of behavior towards others.
- Be a coach.

> *People are not an asset, not a resource. They are a treasure to be protected.*
>
> W. Edwards Deming

Coaching encompasses effective communication and motivation of employees and helping them learn new skills and techniques. It is a way to rapidly transfer skills, knowledge, and experience to people and to encourage them to perform to the best of their ability. The advantages of coaching are: more creativity, more teamwork, motivated employees, and higher productivity. To be able to coach effectively, the following conditions must be present:

- An atmosphere which is non-threatening.
- A climate of openness, trust, and respect.
- Helpfulness and sympathy.
- A personal dialogue focussed on cooperation and teamwork.
- A focus on goals, evaluation of improvements, and feedback on behavior.
- Willingness of others to accept responsibilities for the delegated tasks.

Coaching is also strongly related to delegating, or giving another responsibility and power. A good coach or manager lets others largely do the work. Reasons why managers usually do not delegate are (Thomas, 1995):

- They wish to exercise authority and control.
- Lack of confidence in the ability of the other.
- Fear that the other will do it better.
- The manager wants to attract the attention of his superiors.
- The manager likes to do certain tasks on his own.
- Thinking that he can do it better.
- The opinion that the job is too important to take risks.

Continuous improvement requires leadership on all levels and in all sections of the organization. Everyone in the organization should be a leader. The more leaders who are created, the more successful TQM will be in an organization. That is why authority and responsibility should be given where it is most logical. It is known that people will contribute most when they are responsible for something and have the authority to act. This follows from the needs triangle of Maslow (1970). This triangle shows that people have different kind of needs, and that these determine their behavior (see figure 5.4).

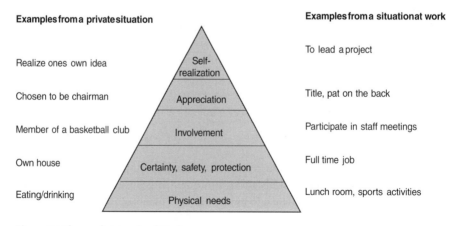

Figure 5.4 The needs trinagle of Maslow

Coaching also involves *empowerment* or giving employees authority, freedom, trust, and information within a fixed framework, make them accept responsibility, and develop skills in order to let them take independent decisions to improve their performance. Some important characteristics of empowered employees are that they:

- Feel responsible for their own work.
- Are given a free hand in their work.
- Balance their own goals with those of the organization.
- Are critical, have self-esteem, and are motivated.
- Are well trained, equipped, creative, and customer oriented.
- Are challenged and encouraged.
- Monitor and improve their work continuously.
- Find new goals and change challenges.

Therefore, it is important to empower individuals and teams on all levels and sections of the organization, by providing them with the necessary authority to meet their responsibility for continuous process improvement.

> *We need to be led by a vision of the future as opposed to being pushed by the problems of the present.*
>
> Methodist Bishop

5.5.1 Four learning styles

To be able to coach teams successfully, managers must ensure that the activities of employees correspond with their learning style. Everyone has his or her own favorite learning style. Based on research done by Honey and Mumford (1992), four methods of learning can be distinguished:

1. The *activist.* Yields completely to new experiences, is broad minded and enthusiastic about everything that is new. Has the tendency to act first and then consider the consequences. As soon as the initial excitement of an activity has faded, he is already looking for something new. He is quickly bored with implementation and consolidation. He is constantly busy with others but makes sure that he stays in the center of activity.
2. The *analyst.* Willingly takes distance to observe things from different angles. Gathers data from experiences and events, considers these profoundly and delays drawing a definite conclusion. Carefully considers all possible angles and implications before taking action. They are cautious people who like to study all possible consequences before acting. They prefer to remain in the background during meetings and discussions and enjoy watching other people work. They are usually detached, tolerant, and inconspicuous in the group.

3. The *theorist.* Adjusts his observations and combines them into a logical theory. Likes to analyze and adores principles, theories, models, and systematic thinking. Solves problems step by step with a consistent logic. He frequently asks: "how does this correspond with that?" and "from what do you draw this?". He dislikes subjectivity and ambiguousness and prefers certainty. He tends to be a perfectionist on the level of arranging things in a rational scheme.
4. The *pragmatist.* Ever so much wants to try ideas, theories, and techniques to see if they work in practice. Is practical and sober and likes to take decisions and solve problems. He gets nervous from endless discussions. He is practical by nature with "both feet on the ground". He sees chances and problems as a challenge. His motto is: "if it only works" and "there always must be a better way". People with this style learn mostly from activities with practical advantages and little theory.

To illustrate the four learning styles, an exercise is shown in table 5.7 to help you discover your favorite learning style (Thomas, 1995). Indicate the learning style that suits you best.

Table 5.7. Which learning style do you prefer?

When you're going to buy a new personal computer, what do you like to do?
(A) Before you use it, take the envelope with "read this first" on it and first read the instructions and directions for use carefully.
(B) Press the salesman to give you an extensive demonstration and to allow you to operate it by yourself, before you decide to buy it. When installing and operating the machine, the instruction manual is next to you.
(C) Don't bother with anything. Just let the equipment be wrapped and play with it. You will soon find out how it works. You have no time to look through the complex instruction manual.
(D) There are a few similarities between this machine and its predecessor, which you recognize. Now you can concentrate on the new elements, try to figure out how it works and then experiment with it. Later you'll read the manual to check if you were correct.
(A) = theorist   (B) = analyst   (C) = activist   (D) = pragmatist

It is to be recommended that you illustrate your own learning style in a diagram and discuss this in your group. From the example in figure 5.5, it is clear that the person is mainly an analyst and a theorist.

5.5.2 How to coach the four learning styles

The coach must understand which needs play an important role in each of the four styles, in order to guarantee that indeed there is learning (Thomas, 1995). This is illustrated in table 5.8.

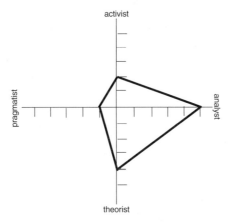

Figure 5.5 Learning styles

Table 5.8 Coaching four learning styles

Activist	Analyst
Support his enthusiasm, but stimulate him to plan in advance. Offer him a diversity of interesting tasks.	Allow him time to prepare himself, to absorb things and study the alternatives.
Theorist	Pragmatist
Give him time to study everything and to draw conclusions. Give him also the opportunity to ask questions, and give him clear objectives and complex ideas to work on.	Give him the chance to plan implementations, and give him the possibilities to practice and provide information and techniques.

5.5.3 Four types of behavior

Besides the learning styles of employees, the coach must also consider their behavior. In general, people are divided into the following behavioral categories (Thomas, 1995 and Geier & Downey, 1989):

1. The *dominant-directive type.* These people are driven by an internal need to lead, to take things into their own hands to achieve their goals. They have a clear opinion, self-esteem, a positive self-portrait and a strong ego, love a challenge, have a strong will, independent and goal oriented, they have the tendency to criticize others and traditional working methods, and dislike routine work. They are pragmatic, reactive, and energetic. They like to feel important and like to impress people. They are also opinionated, impatient and hard. They prefer to have control over others and can sometimes hardly endure the feelings, opinions, and shortcomings of others. They usually listen very badly.
2. The *social-interactive type.* These people are talkative, popular, convincing, impulsive, enthusiastic and like to be in the picture. They have a lot of energy

and a need for social acknowledgement and like a loving treatment. They try to influence others in an optimistic and friendly way that is focused on a positive result. What they fear most is public humiliation and they can go to the limit to avoid this. In general, they work supportively, trustingly, intuitively, scoutingly, and conciliatorily towards solving problems. They like brain storming and contacts with colleagues, enjoy it when they don't have to bother with supervision, details, and complex matters and prefer to participate in important projects and activities. Their weak points are a lack of patience, and limited power of concentration. They are quickly bored and sometimes neglect to check certain things. When they feel insufficiently involved or stimulated, they are bored and look for a distraction, which can result in superficial, inconstant, and excessive emotional behavior.

3. The ***uniform-stable type.*** These people are quiet, calm, loyal, predictable, patient, persevering, go-getters, result-oriented, laconic, and modest. They don't express themselves easily and prefer a slower and easier pace than others, and are eager to finish things. They concentrate on building trust and strive for sustainable personal relationships and preservation of a stable and well-balanced environment. They are friendly, helpful, and seldom show rage or euphoria. They dislike sudden changes. Every interference with their fixed working method can make them lose their composure. They solve problems by observing and thinking about them as well as applying solutions. They dislike taking risks and prefer repetitive activities. They also respect traditions, feel uncomfortable with conflicts and enjoy formulating rules and implementing them.

4. The ***thoughtful type.*** These people are accurate, reliable, independent, careful, detached, introverts, inventive, perfectionists, and resourceful. They take little risks, prefer to have clearly divined priorities, want to know which pace is expected of them, and are eager to know how something works in order to judge everything correctly. Because they uphold their own norms and values, they expect a lot from themselves and others. They will only go into action when they have determined which tasks and aspects will actually influence the desired results. Sometimes it can take a while before they raise certain matters, because they usually need additional actual information.

It is recommended that you also illustrate your type of behavior in a diagram and discuss it in your group. From the example in figure 5.6, it is clear that the person is mainly a thoughtful type.

> *The leader of the future pays much attention to issues such as fairness, justice, integrity, human dignity, service, and quality.*
>
> Stephen Covey

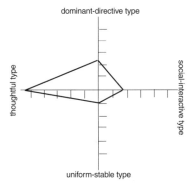

Figure 5.6 Types of behavior

5.5.4 How to coach the four types of behavior

The manager has to understand which types of behavior are in his team or section, in order to coach his employees effectively. A couple of interesting suggestions for successful coaching of employees are shown in table 5.9 for each type of behavior (Thomas, 1995).

Table 5.9 How to coach the four types of behavior

Dominant-directive type	*Social-interactive type*
– show them how to win; give them new possibilities – bring variety in their way of working and look for possibilities to create variation – give evidence of logic reasoning and develop their listening skills by letting them, for example, repeat their own words and what was agreed upon – give brief information, facts, and crucial points – make agreements about the goals and let it be confirmed verbally – allow them to take initiatives within the correct borders – make them conscious of the effects of rushed conclusions – pay attention to what they have achieved and compliment them about it – give them the lead when it is appropriate, but give them relevant data – enter a discussion about a topic that you disagree on with conviction and positive attitude, but based on facts and not on opinions – help them to be more considerate to the feelings of others	– support their need for approval and making a good impression, by enthusiastically expressing your believe in their ideas and your support to them – avoid complex details – give evidence of logic reasoning and increase their listening skills by stimulating them to repeat everything that has been discussed in their own words – help them to draft a coherent plan to obtain results based on objectives – set limits to time available for discussions and tasks – make the job changeable and avoid tasks with repetitions – give them your sincere appreciation and compliment them on their performance and improvements – execute tasks together with them and coach them in logical decision-making so that their ideas are converted into tangible results – don't be aggressive and avoid personal discussions – be active, stimulating, and keep a high pace

Table 5.9 (Continued)

Uniform-stable type	Thoughtful type
– warn them in advance of eventual changes and new assignments – convince them with logic reasoning and provide the necessary information and proof – show that you are interested in them – give clear instructions and descriptions – compliment them for their patience and perseverance – don't behave aggressive towards them and avoid conflicts – provide a relaxed and friendly working environment – acknowledge their helpful manner and give feedback at the right time	– approach them in an indirect, non-aggressive and careful way – show the reasons for certain decisions, explain and give an interpretation of the underlying principles – let them study the improvements and results of others before they take their own decision – compliment them on their thorough and correct way of working – request additional explanations and assistance in preventing conflicts and resistance – allow them time to philosophize, reflect, and look for the correct answer within the available limits.

5.5.5 Four culture elements

The four mentioned types of behavior are related to the following culture elements: earth, water, air, and fire. These primeval elements have a symbolic meaning. Thus, earth means: soil under the feet, a foundation to build on. Water relates to fertility, life, refreshment, trend, following the stream, cooling, flood, devastation. Air encompasses space, liveability, and dynamics. Fire regards warmth, energy, light, adventure, danger, and destruction. These elements are displayed in table 5.10 (van der Loo, 1995).

Table 5.10 Four culture elements

Earth	Water	Air	Fire
Involved	Expectant	Flexible	Active
Idealistic	Precise/perseverance	Creative	Energetic
Sincere	Careful/quiet	Inquisitive	Guiding
Perfectionist	Business-like	Inventive/innovative	Target oriented
Fundamental	Avoid risks	Spontaneous	Active
Cooperative	Calm and quiet	Impulsive	Performance oriented
Tender	Detached	Optimistic	Focused on the big issue
Considerate	Formal	Witty	Quick decisive
Helpful	Look at the facts	Complimentary	Strong-willed
Introvert	Sensitive to procedures	Extravert/communicative	Direct
Encourage unity	Methodical	Intuitive	Adventurous/change oriented

The culture elements can also be displayed in a diagram (figure 5.7). From this example, it is clear that the person is an earth type.

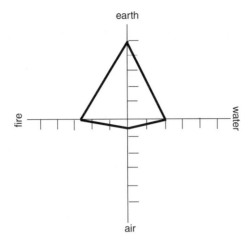

Figure 5.7 Culture elements

World class leaders:
- *Are personally committed to quality.*
- *Fully understand key processes.*
- *Focus on tangible process measurements.*
- *Believe in teamwork and empowerment.*
- *Compare their processes against the "best in the world".*
- *Are involved and available.*
- *Are generally curious.*
- *Are personally committed to learning and teaching.*

Bruce Gissing, Vice-president Operations, Boeing

5.5.6 Four leadership styles

The effectiveness of a leader is not only determined by personal characteristics and behavior, but also by the degree to which the style of management is adjusted to the situation. There are two basic dimensions of leaders, namely: focus on tasks (work that has to be accomplished), and focus on relations. When focusing on tasks, managers mainly concentrate on structuring tasks which need to be accomplished. Thus, indicating what and how the job must be done. In this case, it means:

- Determining measurable goals for employees.
- Organizing and distributing work.
- Providing adequate resources.
- Instructing employees how to execute their job.
- Checking the quality of work.

When focusing on relations, managers mainly concentrate on the needs and wishes of the individual. This implies improving the satisfaction of employees. In this case, it means:

- Expressing appreciation for the employees.
- Providing support when necessary.
- Looking for tasks which fit the capacities and ambitions of the employees.
- Stimulating mutual deliberations and teamwork.

In general, four leadership styles are distinguished. Please refer to table 5.11

Table 5.11 Four leadership styles

Crafty	*Organizational*
- the boss knows and directs everything - the boss is the query box for his subordinates and he dictates what they must do - he punishes and rewards as he pleases - the boss acts intuitively, mostly out of short term motives - the boss elaborates on old proven methods	- the chief organizes work, is work oriented and directs from a distance - he shows how a problem can be solved and monitors progress - the chief evaluates the employees based on established criteria - he lets arguments determine the decision making - the chief decides based on long term goals - he is open to innovations
Situation- oriented	*Entrepreneurial*
- the leader knows it, but mobilizes his employees - he keeps an eye on the processes - the leader asks questions in such a way that the employees discover solutions by themselves - he follows the developments, gives instructions, guides, and supports where necessary - the leader appreciates efforts of employees and rewards based on performance - the leader develops the qualities of the employees - he forms a bridge between old and new working methods - he creates autonomy with a coordinated coherence	- is forward-looking - is creative - takes well thought-out risks - has a vision of the future - can communicate well - identifies important trends - anticipates changes - is people oriented - establishes goals - he feels personally responsible - wants to produce something

It is recommended that you also illustrate your leadership style in a diagram and discuss this in your organization. Ask your employees on which points you're not clear enough and try to change that. A profile of a leader is shown in figure 5.8. From this example, it is clear that this leader is mainly organizational and entrepreneurial in nature.

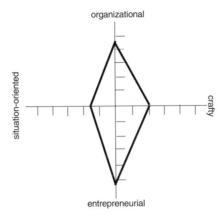

Figure 5.8 Leadership styles

> *Leaders create the vision, articulate the vision, passionately own the vision, and relentlessly drive it to completion.*
>
> Jack Welch, President General Electric

5.5.7 Eight leadership roles

Effective leaders are people who can perform different roles. Quinn (1996) distinguishes the following roles: *producer, director, coordinator, checker, stimulator, mentor, innovator,* and *negotiator* (see table 5.12 and figure 5.9). All these roles are strongly related to each other and can be contrary to each other, but can also supplement each other.

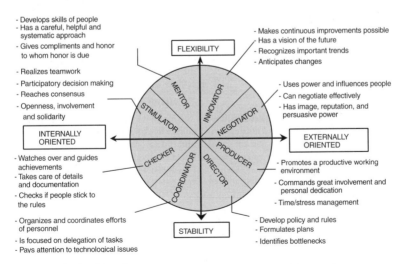

Figure 5.9 Eight leadership roles

Table 5.12 Eight leadership roles

Producer	Director
It is expected of a producer that he promotes a productive working environment, that he is deeply involved, motivated and devoted, accepts responsibilities, and transforms assignments into acceptable results. For the manager as a producer, the only criteria for effectiveness of the organization are productivity and profits.	The director determines the goals, chooses the right strategy, makes expectations clear, determines the policy and rules, identifies bottlenecks, selects solutions, defines tasks, and gives instructions. Thus, he is the designer of the organization. For a manager as a director, the only criteria for effectiveness of the organization are productivity and profits. When taking a decision, the final result and maximum output are mainly considered. Employees are only rewarded when they highly contribute to the realization of these goals.
Coordinator	**Checker**
The manager as coordinator is mainly concentrated on delegating tasks through the organization and arrangement of efforts of personnel, and managing crises. He pays much attention to technological and domestic issues. The leader in this role must be trustworthy and reliable. The coordinator emphasizes maintenance and consolidation of processes, whereby conduct of business management is mainly characterized by a hierarchical and bureaucratic structure.	The manager as a checker knows what is going on in the company, checks if the employees stick to the rules, takes care of details, settles the administration and documentation, and does inspection rounds. The emphasis of the checker is on maintenance and consolidation of processes, whereby management is mainly characterized by a hierarchical and bureaucratic structure.
Stimulator	**Mentor**
From a manager as a stimulator is expected that he stimulates cooperation, involvement, and solidarity, realizes teamwork, solves problems between employees, contributes to the moral development, displays great openness and knows how to reach consensus. This leader is a coach, guide, and companion. He can initiate learning processes and strengthen the collective power of employees. The stimulator appreciates people because they are people.	The manager as a mentor is mainly focused on the development of employee skills through a careful, helpful, and sympathetic approach. He also listens to his employees, expresses his appreciation, and gives compliments. The mentor (teacher) helps employees structure their vision so that they can look beyond superficial circumstances. The mentor values people because they are people. Conduct of business management is mainly internally focused and flexible. Development of human resources and cultural change is central here.
Innovator	**Negotiator**
The manager as an innovator makes continuous improvements possible, has a strategic vision of the future, recognizes important trends and demands in the market, sees ways to satisfy these demands, anticipates changes which are necessary, has insight into the demands of customers and tolerates risks. Above all things, they are creative and clever people, who can see into the future. With the innovator, competitive position, expansion, continuous improvement, adaptability, innovation, and creative solving of problems are central.	The manager as a negotiator is politically conscious, uses his power and influence to obtain resources from outside and can negotiate effectively. Reputation and image are very important here. This manager usually acts as a go-between and spokesman.

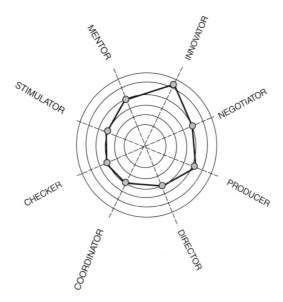

Figure 5.10 Eight leadership roles

Successful managers have the ability to fulfill all mentioned roles in an optimal mix, and balance these.

Illustrate in a diagram which roles you fulfil and discuss this in your organization. Ask your employees which roles you fulfill insufficiently and try to make changes. The profile of a leader is shown in figure 5.10. From this example, it is evident that this leader fulfills the different roles in a good combination. He is mainly an innovator.

> *Treat your employees exactly as you want them to treat your best customers.*
>
> Stephen Covey

5.5.8 Recommendations for effective leadership

John Gardner (1990) states a number of leadership attributes which apply to leaders in both the public and private sector (see table 5.13). Table 5.13 displays a summarized review of the most important activities/characteristics of an effective leader.

Table 5.13 John Gardner's Attributes of Leadership

ATTRIBUTE	WHAT IT MEANS
Physical vitality and stamina	You have a high energy level and are physically durable.
Intelligence and judgment-in-action	You can combine hard data, questionable data, and intuitive guesses to arrive at a conclusion that events prove to be correct.
Willingness(eagerness) to accept responsibilities	You have an impulse to exercise initiative in social situations. You step forward when no one else will.
Task competence	You have knowledge of the task at hand.
Understanding of followers/constituents and their needs	You understand the various constituencies with whom you work.
Skill in dealing with people	You can appraise accurately the readiness or resistance of followers to move in a given direction. You make the most of their motives and understand their sensitivities.
Need to achieve	You have a driving pressure to achieve.
Capacity to motivate	You communicate persuasively. You move people to action.
Courage, resolution, steadiness	You are willing to take risks. You never give up. You stay the course.
Capacity to win and hold trust	You have an extraordinary ability to win the trust of people.
Capacity to manage, decide, set priorities	You perform the traditional task of management – formulating goals, setting priorities, framing a course of action, selecting aides, and delegating-very well.
Confidence	You continually nominate yourself for leadership tasks. You have confidence that others will react positively to your offer of leadership.
Ascendance, dominance, assertiveness	You have a strong impulse to take charge.
Adaptability, flexibility of approach	You can shift swiftly and without hesitation from a failing tactic to another approach, and if that does not work, to still another.

Source: John Gardner, On Leadership, Free Press, New York, 1990, pp. 48-53.

Table 5.14 Activities/characteristics of an effective leader

Is proactive, modest, not arrogant, and a servant.
Listens effectively and is creative.
Foresees things and can anticipate the unexpected.
Focuses on e-business.
Uses information of suppliers and customers systematically for improvement of critical processes.
Is on call for all employees and inspires them.
Considers personal circumstances.
Delegates in confidence, gives responsibility and power.
Displays an ambitious vision and mission and communicates these consistently to his employees with conviction.
Has developed his own personal vision statement, which is consistent with that of the entire organization.
Shows involvement, gives room, admits confidence and gives clear acknowledgement and appreciates the performance of his employees.
Is the embodiment of peace, is visible, and communicates consistently and preferably face to face.
Creates clearness about tasks and positions, and gives constructive feedback.
Is open and honest without hidden agendas.
Takes initiative to lead, and well thought out risks, is innovative, dares to accept mistakes, and does the right thing.
Sometimes offers to help with the daily work of the employees, without checking them and interfering with details.
Maintains and promotes relations with employees, customers and suppliers with understanding.
Promotes multidisciplinary teamwork and creates involvement and active participation of everyone.
Cultivates mutual respect and trust. Relies on trust.
Creates situations in which there is no fear of improvements, people are happy and proud of their work, and in which people are responsible for their work and that of others.
Creates an environment in which continuous improvement is "a way of life".
Demonstrates a belief in and commitment to continuous improvement on all levels of the organization and functions as the process owner.
Trusts his own instincts and intuition as strongly as facts and analyses.
Has the ability to determine which direction the organization should go and the ability to distinguish between ideals and hard facts. Has his priorities well established and takes consistent decisions.
Stimulates employees to take initiatives and to take a liable position towards customers.
Inspires employees to set concrete, feasible, and measurable goals, to realize those, and to change.
Recognizes specific individual contributions to improvement efforts; if employees generate ideas, they are praised; if they identify problems, they are thanked; when they contribute, they are recognized; when they fail, they are supported; and when they succeed, they are rewarded.
Recognizes that people are the most important treasure. Focuses on people.
Establishes channels of communication, which are reliable and accessible to everyone in the organization.
Takes regular strolls in the department and chats with the employees.
Has conversations with customers and inquires about their expectations.

Table 5.14 (Continued)

Continuously does benchmarking and creates new learning effects through innovation.
Shows employees how their activities contribute to the larger picture.
Develops and uses performance indicators which are related to critical processes.
Regularly organizes meetings and workshops to create clearness about the firm's policy, the core values of the organization, and the TQM approach.
Stimulates employees to participate in training, directs this, and offers support during training

As a practical follow up to the leadership concepts and characteristics, I present the Philips Quality Leadership Role Model in the following frame (Philips, Electronics, 1993). This model is a comprehensive description of the variety of tasks to be accomplished by all Philips managers in order to ensure the implementation of Philips Quality in their area of responsibility. It is used:

- as a source of inspiration in discussions of management teams;
- as a guideline for directing individual and team actions;
- as a support of management education;
- as a reference for appraisal and recognition of managers;
- as an input for action planning on management development.

> **Philips Quality Leadership Role Model**
>
> **The customer first**
>
> Listen to customers and actively seek their opinion on the value of the products and services supplied. Make the customer visible, especially to those who are not in day-to-day contact with customers. Where relevant develop a close link with customers and seek joint improvement activity. Lead the handling of complaints.
>
> **Demonstrate involvement**
>
> Introduce and apply the Philips Quality principles and methodology. Participate in improvement activities and teamwork. Demonstrate the value of new methods and techniques. Benchmark the quality process.
>
> **Value people and foster teamwork**
>
> Take care of the development of people's skills and capabilities. Train for Philips Quality and coach the application. Enable people to be responsible for the result of their work. Monitor, appraise and recognize people's performance. Advance teamwork and put team success ahead of individual achievement.
>
> **Build supplier partnership**
>
> Clarify Philips Quality to suppliers, audit their capabilities, give feedback, discuss improvements and support them where needed. Recognize quality improvements made by suppliers and encourage joint improvement action.
>
> **Strive for excellence**
>
> Hold the Philips Quality path, review progress of the improvement process and use conclusions to plan new initiatives. Actively seek best practices and use these to strengthen the approach.
>
> **Explain and deploy policy**
>
> Explain the quality policy, as part of the business policy, to all involved. Set stretching targets and deploy these to business processes, to the functions within the organization, and to suppliers.
>
> **Manage improvement trough processes**
>
> Demonstrate that the functional organization produces value for customers through processes. Make processes visible and manageable. Assess capabilities and measure performance. Seek ownership for process improvement and for process re-design.

> *Above all, quality requires leadership..........Leadership is needed to make things happen...........*
> *Our role is to provide the vision and the leadership, to set goals, conduct managerial audits, monitor customer satisfaction and employee morale, participate in quality training, act as coaches and evaluate managers on these criteria.*
>
> Jan D. Timmer, former President Philips Electronics

To illustrate the foregoing, an updated profile of the new maintenance chief of Oil Refinery Shell Pernis at Rotterdam is shown in table 5.15.

Table 5.15   Updated profile of Oil Refinery Shell Pernis new maintenance chiefs

Key points: the new manager is a coach, has to set an example, and strives continuously for top quality in everything he/she does.

ATTITUDE AND TASKS	SKILLS
– Is honest, trustworthy, and consistent	– Can listen well
– Is part of the team	– Can carry out norms and values so that a "we feeling" develops
– Is open for other opinions	– Can take decisions and carry these through
– Respects the individual	
– Delegates in confidence and directs where necessary	– Can collaborate harmoniously, as well as transfer and mobilize knowledge and skills
– Balances his own personal mission and vision with those of his team	– Can handle constructive confrontations
– Is client-oriented, goal-oriented, performance- oriented, energetic, and change oriented	– Can plan, command, and improve activities
– Is continuously focused on the development and mobilization of the employee's knowledge	– Can distinguish the important from the less important
– Inspires employees to set goals and to realize these	– Can communicate clearly, and openly at the right moment
– Lays down borders within which team members can take independent decisions	– Can create circumstances in which people are productive and in which people are responsible for their own work and that of others
– Takes well thought-out risks, is innovative, and dares to accept mistakes	– Has a talent to identify trends and to anticipate them early
– Is patient and resolute	– Can activate, stimulate, and motivate people
– Is positive and enthusiastic	– Can maintain tranquility in the organization
– Has guts (sticks his neck out), and continuously takes initiatives	
– Keeps appointments and shows drive to obtain results	– Can judge and develop competence
– Has perseverance and convincing power	– Can create cultural change, focused on hard work, teamwork, and active participation of everyone
– Is stress proof and radiates peace	
– Has a sense of responsibility and takes initiatives (is proactive)	– Can translate strategic policy plans into tasks and goals and visa versa
– He displays a vision and carries this out in an active way	– Has a lot of experience in the respective field.
– Shows involvement, gives room and is visible	

Table 5.15 (Continued)

– Promotes teamwork based on respect for each other – Shows appreciation for contributions of others – Creates a climate of openness and trust – Is human oriented, learns from his/her mistakes, strives for consensus, lets arguments determine the decision-making and is completely devoted to the common goal.
KNOWLEDGE: is deep enough, broad, up to date, and links to the employee's knowledge level

The most important characteristics of effective teamwork can be summarized as follows: discussing, deciding, and doing the work together, democratic decision making, no personal conflicts, group interest and own interest are an extension of each other, team goals are linked to the organizational goals, everyone knows what to stick to, the team leader coaches, directs, guides, and develops the team as a whole and encourages open discussions, the team leader makes optimal use of the skills of team members, there is a fruitful collaboration whereby there is a breakthrough of deadlocks, there is a broad basis of trust, there is a brotherly atmosphere, they accept each other, there are no status barriers and hidden agendas, people learn from mistakes, active participation from all team members, team members take initiatives and offer suggestions for improvements, there is a tight link within the group and they take each other into consideration, new team members are accepted and mentored without problems, opposing opinions are open for discussion, are being discussed and lead to improvements, irritations are being discussed, they correct each other if necessary, the members are willing to make concessions for the benefit of the team, the team directs itself, team members have a feeling of being accepted and having power, the functioning of the team is continuously being evaluated, and quality improvement techniques from the problem solving discipline are systematically implemented, as well as the earlier mentioned interpersonal skills. For the benefit of effective teamwork, it is also important to limit the meetings of improvement teams to one and a half hour, every week on the same day, time and place (especially in the initial phase) and to evaluate teamwork regularly.

Management is to do things right. Leadership is to do good things............ *Efficient management without effective leadership is a waist of time.........* *First, leadership is required and then management.*   Peter Drucker & Warren Bennis

6 The Quality Improvement Process

The fourth pillar of the TQM-house (see figure 6.1) encompasses the Quality Improvement Process (QIP), which is a technique to work systematically, disciplined, and as a team towards continuous quality improvement of the entire organization. It is a method to establish systematic, continuous, and gradual improvement towards total quality. To realize total quality, everyone within the organization should consider continuous improvement as something normal. Continuous improvement of the organization is one of the basics of total quality. Teamwork, interpersonal skills, and the correct implementation of the explained methods and techniques are necessary for continuous improvement.

> *Don't bother just to be better than your contemporaries or predecessors. Try to be better than yourself.*
>
> William Faulkner

Figure 6.2 illustrates how the different QIP- parts are related. This model provides you with a plan for identifying and defining your processes, identifying improvement opportunities, standardizing the current best-known way of executing your processes, and implementing and evaluating improvement efforts. The QIP can be divided into four steps:

- Process selection
- Process evaluation
- Process standardization
- Process improvement

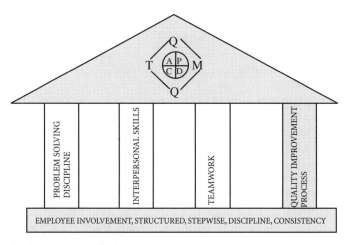

Figure 6.1 The fourth pillar of the TQM-house

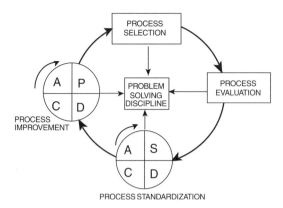

Figure 6.2 The quality improvement process

These activities are executed with the assistance of the Problem Solving Discipline (PSD). By continuously working as a team according to the QIP-model and adopting the quality mentality and quality skills, you'll be able to improve your organization continuously. Mistakes will be eliminated systematically and as a result, employees will speak the same "quality language". To achieve this, it is necessary that everyone within the organization continuously make use of the PSD and the QIP.

6.1 Process selection

In the first step of the QIP (see figure 6.3), the emphasis is on defining the product or service and the customer's needs, making an inventory of customer's data and complaints, and selecting processes which cause most of these complaints. The central questions in this case are:

1. Which products or services do we provide?
2. Who are our customers?
3. What do they want, what are their requirements?
4. Is it measurable?
5. Which critical processes need improvement?

By answering these questions continuously, the customer will be better understood, and the product or service will be better in tune with the market demand.

Which products/services do we provide?

First of all, define your most important product or service as concretely as possible. This definition must indicate what you're really doing as a supplier. The more specific the definition, the better the customer's needs can be met.

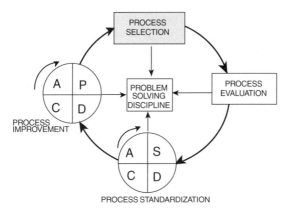

Figure 6.3 Step one in the quality improvement process

Who are our customers?

It is important for TQM to understand the entire chain of customers. This means that you should know all of your customers. The needs of each customer must be examined separately. Not only the external, but also the internal customers should be considered. In fact, if the company does not satisfy the needs of the internal customers, how will they be able to comply with the needs of the external customer? All employees determine the degree of customer satisfaction. Employees from within different departments must be considered customers of each other. By bringing individual employees together as customers and suppliers, the traditional barriers between departments will be broken. Each employee delivers something to a colleague, whereby one functions as the internal supplier and the other as the internal customer.

Figure 6.4 shows that department C functions as the internal customer of department B, and department A as the internal supplier of department B. Strengthening this relationship results in an internal network of customer/supplier relationships, which is beneficial to the quality of services provided to the external customer. Everyone in the organization must learn to think in terms of: *Who is my customer and how can I satisfy his/her needs?*

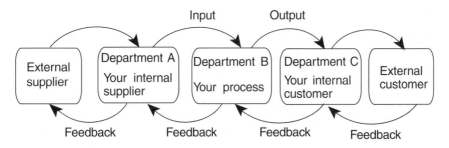

Figure 6.4 Customer-Supplier-Relationship

To illustrate this approach, the "Hewlard-Packards" internal customer checklist is shown below (Rees, et al., 1988). The assumption here is that each part of the organization should ask itself seven questions which it regards as fundamental to the operation.

HEWLETT PACKARD'S INTERNAL CUSTOMER CHECKLIST
1. Who are my customers?
2. What do they need?
3. What is my product or service?
4. What are my customers' expectations and measures?
5. Does my product or service meet their expectations?
6. What is the process for providing my product or service?
7. What action is required to improve the process?

Problem-solving methodology

1. Select the quality issue	8. Identify the major causes of the quality
2. Write an issue statement	9. Plan for improvements
3. Identify the process	10. Take the corrective action
4. Draw a flow chart	11. Collect and analyse the data again
5. Select a process performance measure	12. Are the objectives met?
6. Conduct a cause and effect analysis	13. If yes, document and standardize the change
7. Collect and analyse the data	

What do they want, what are their requirements?

As a supplier, you should try to figure out what the customer needs and wants. Communication is very important. Talk to your customers and ask them what they think of your product or service. Try to figure out how they use it and what they really want. Listen especially to what they have to say and indicate which customer-supplier relationship needs improvements. The central questions hereby are:

- Which needs and expectations do your customers have?
- Which needs and expectations are you aware of?
- To what extend do you comply with the needs and expectations of your customers?
- If you do not satisfy their needs, what are the reasons according to your customers?

Making an inventory of customer's data, customer's complaints, and benchmarking are important opportunities to improve the customer orientation of the organization. Information about the opinion of the customer regarding your product or service is of essential importance, and can be obtained in several ways, such as customer surveys, phone interviews, and customer panel discussions. Customer surveys are a powerful tool to get information about what the customer thinks and expects. In general, questionnaires are used with different questions, which may vary from organization to organization. The exhibit below lists a number of clues about how to correctly formulate these questions (Philips Electronics, 1994).

How do you formulate your questions?

- Ask questions which can lead to action. You have to be able to do something with the reply.
- Ask answerable questions. The customer must be able to know the answer to the question.
- Ask clear questions. The customer should not be in doubt about the meaning or the intention of the question. Be specific. Do not ask complicated questions which require more than one sentence.
- Avoid too much detail. You can always ask a number of customers after the survey has been completed to give you some additional clarification.
- Ask questions which have only a limited number of answers. It allows the customer to answer quickly and accurately.
- The customer must consider the questions relevant. Don't include a specific subject which is of less importance to the customer in a customer satisfaction survey.
- Ask the customer about his overall satisfaction. For example: *consider all these aspects, what is your overall satisfaction with the suppliers we have discussed here?*
- The last question is for the customer. At the end of the survey, always ask which subject the customer has missed in the survey which he feels is important.
- Keep it short. Answering all the questions should not take more than 15 minutes. If you make the list longer, then customers may become irritable and rush through the answers.

As an example, a questionnaire from Occidental Hotels is shown in table 6.1, in which complaints from the hotel guests are systematically registered. To illustrate a customer oriented approach, a satisfaction measurement for an installation company is shown in table 6.2. Complaints of customers must be considered to be something positive, as a chance to learn from mistakes and to improve the process or product in such a way that the complaints do not reoccur. Complaints of customers form an important source of information for improvement. After the customer's data are collected, they must be analyzed to be able to improve your product or service and the related processes.

Customers are funny, they don't always tell you they are dissatisfied with your service, they just go elsewhere.

Deise, M.V. et al., 2000

Table 6.1 Questionnaire Occidental Hotels

Please rate the following aspects:	Very important	Fairly important	Without importance	COMPLETELY SATISFIED	VERY SATISFIED	SATISFIED	FAIRLY SATISFIED	UNSATISFIED
1) ATTENTION								
A) Friendliness of the staff at the:								
– Front Desk	☐	☐	☐	○	○	○	○	○
– Restaurants	☐	☐	☐	○	○	○	○	○
– Bars	☐	☐	☐	○	○	○	○	○
– Housekeeping	☐	☐	☐	○	○	○	○	○
– Maintenance	☐	☐	☐	○	○	○	○	○
– Amusement club	☐	☐	☐	○	○	○	○	○
Comments: _____								
B) Staff efficiency at the:								
– Front Desk	☐	☐	☐	○	○	○	○	○
– Restaurants	☐	☐	☐	○	○	○	○	○
– Bars	☐	☐	☐	○	○	○	○	○
– Housekeeping	☐	☐	☐	○	○	○	○	○
– Maintenance	☐	☐	☐	○	○	○	○	○
Comments: _____								
C) Communication and co-operation concerning your needs at the:								
– Front Desk	☐	☐	☐	○	○	○	○	○
– Restaurants	☐	☐	☐	○	○	○	○	○
– Bars	☐	☐	☐	○	○	○	○	○
– Amusement club	☐	☐	☐	○	○	○	○	○
Comments: _____								
2) AMUSEMENT CLUB								
– Variety	☐	☐	☐	○	○	○	○	○
– Suitability	☐	☐	☐	○	○	○	○	○
Comments: _____								

Table 6.1 (Continued)

Please rate the following aspects:	Very important	Fairly important	Without importance	COMPLETELY SATISFIED	VERY SATISFIED	SATISFIED	FAIRLY SATISFIED	UNSATISFIED
3) FOOD AND BEVERAGE **A) Variety at:**								
– Restaurants	☐	☐	☐	○	○	○	○	○
– Buffets	☐	☐	☐	○	○	○	○	○
– Bars	☐	☐	☐	○	○	○	○	○
Comments: _____								
B) Presentation at:								
– Restaurants	☐	☐	☐	○	○	○	○	○
– Buffets	☐	☐	☐	○	○	○	○	○
– Bars	☐	☐	☐	○	○	○	○	○
Comments: _____								
4) FACILITIES **A) Cleanliness in:**								
– Rooms	☐	☐	☐	○	○	○	○	○
– Public areas	☐	☐	☐	○	○	○	○	○
– Bars	☐	☐	☐	○	○	○	○	○
– Swimming-pool area	☐	☐	☐	○	○	○	○	○
Comments: _____								
B) Overall standards and maintenance of the hotel:	☐	☐	☐	○	○	○	○	○
Comments: _____								
5) GENERAL SATISFACTION – Taking everything into consideration, how would you rate your stay with us?				○	○	○	○	○

Why _____

What did you appreciate most? _____

Is there anything that didn't meet your expectations _____

What did you find lacking? _____

Would you like to mention any member of our staff? _____

In your opinion, would you consider coming back to our hotel in the future? Yes Maybe No

Table 6.2 Satisfaction measurement for an installation company

Satisfaction characteristics	Completely	Fairly	Not really	Not at all	Importance 1 = unimportant 5 = very important
Answer possibilities					
Delivers the work neatly					
Has polite employees					
Delivers the work at the agreed upon time					
Is a reliable company					
Has a good idea about the customers requirements					
Continues searching for the best solution					
Deliver quality that matches the expectation of the customer					
Is easily reachable (by phone)					
Give good work guarantee					
Mechanics are well prepared for their tasks					
Complaints are handled in an expert way					
Failures and urgent repairs are solved quickly					
Maintains an adequate relationship with customers					

Some important recommendations to improve your customer orientation are:

- Link your personal and organizational mission and vision statement to customer satisfaction.
- Identify external and internal customers.
- Establish a routine and meaningful dialogue with customers.
- Listen effectively to your customers, and treat each customer as unique.
- Introduce a customer's helpdesk or a call center.
- Regularly organize meetings with groups of customers to let them inform you about their needs, wants, ideas, and complaints.
- The organization is within reach and available to customers.
- Continuously train employees in customer orientation.
- Train your customers in TQM, and organize a customer TQM seminar.
- Teach the front line and sales employees how to communicate effectively with customers and based on their reaction, how to act.
- Employees must be willing to help customers. Only satisfied employees can satisfy customers.
- Visit your important customers regularly.
- Organize excursions for your employees to important customers.
- Anticipate customer needs.
- View customer information as strategic asset.

- Routinely conduct customer surveys among your customers about your products and services provided. Feed these results systematically back to the employees to stimulate the improvement process.
- Communicate customers' opinion throughout the company; makes the voice of the customer heard by everyone.
- Introduce a customer hero or a customer champion contest.
- Formulate adequate customer dispatch procedures and implement them.
- Use measured customer friendliness as an indicator of improvement.
- Involve your customers in the development of new products and processes.
- Develop a partnership relation with your customers, based on mutual trust and respect.
- Allow your customers to participate actively in your improvement teams, and involve them in the decision making process.
- Systematically evaluate agreements made with your customers, and communicate these to the stakeholders within the organization.
- Inspire employees to measure their efforts and results against customers' needs and expectations.

Many of these recommendations also apply to your relationships with external suppliers. Treat your suppliers as business partners, as though they are an integral part of your organization. Listen to their ideas on how you can work closely and productively together, create value-added relationships and joint improvement teams with them, invite suggestions from them, assist them in improving their own processes, build mutual trust and respect, reward them if they achieve improvements, let them participate in the celebration of success, involve them in the development of new products & processes, and become a better customer yourself. Use e-business to share business improvements, mutual benefits, and joint rewards. Expanding your culture of continuous improvement to all your suppliers will ensure that the quality of your inputs is sufficient to meet your own improvement objectives. If possible, minimize the number of suppliers; go with the few best and improvement-oriented suppliers with a demonstrated TQM culture and effective leadership by top-management, based on a long term partnership contract.

What the company thinks its customer wants
  is not necessarily the same as

What the company thinks it has to offer
  is not necessarily the same as

What the company actually offers
  is not necessarily the same as

How the customer experiences this
  is not necessarily the same as

What the customer really wants

Philips Electronics

Is it measurable?

To comply with the needs of the customer, it is necessary to translate these into product specifications. *Quality Function Deployment* is a practical technique to do this (see § 3.2.14). Usually, it is necessary to negotiate with the customer, which results in feasible and agreed upon customer's requirements, which are measurable and understood by all parties. All statements of the customer about qualitative aspects must be translated into quantitative specifications for the supplier. Define clearly and explicitly what they are talking about.

The other actions in this first step of the QIP are:

- Select a critical process, which is being considered for improvement, based on the changed value of its performance indicator; this involves identifying all potential opportunities, prioritizing them, and choosing the process which presents the biggest problem or the greatest opportunity for improvement.
- Formulate the mission, vision, core values, goals, and strategies of the organization and build consensus around these. Analyze customer data and complaints.
- Determine the improvement objectives.
- Create commitment at top management.
- Create a working climate which is characterized by teamwork, creativity, mutual respect, and continuous improvement.

The results of this step in the QIP are:

- Increased chances at "right the first time".
- Improved communication between customer and supplier, which results in better understanding.
- Selection of processes which cause most complaints from customers and are being considered for improvement.

A customer satisfaction measurement system is shown in table 6.3, to illustrate the activities developed in this step. This system is partially based on work by Thomassen (1997). Mark a possibility with a cross at each question. Discuss the results of these measurements and check why this customer orientation profile is typical for your organization. Establish a plan to improve your customer service. According to Deise et al. (2000), this can be managed by three main business objectives: 1) increasing customer satisfaction by improving the timeliness and quality of service, 2) reducing the cost of delivering service (by outsourcing to third-party suppliers, reducing the overhead, etc.), and 3) growing service revenue by offering value-adding service offerings in increasingly competitive markets.

Table 6.3 Customer satisfaction measurement

I Customers	Yes	No
1. Do you know who your customers are and how many customers you have?		
2. Do you listen effectively to all your customers?		
3. Do you regularly make up an inventory of all the needs and expectations of your customers?		
4. Did you segment your customers based on their needs?		
5. Do you routinely use questionnaires and conduct surveys among your customers about your products and services?		
6. Are all your employees informed about the results of these questionnaires and surveys?		
7. Are more than 75% of your customers satisfied?		
8. Do you anticipate customer needs?		
9. Do you treat each customer as unique?		
10. Are complaints replied to within two days and solved within one week?		
11. Do you stimulate customers to register their complaints?		
12. Do you use e-business tools to communicate with customers?		
13. Do you have a customer's helpdesk or a call center?		
14. Do you know which percentage of the customers who terminated their relationship with your organization, did this out of dissatisfaction?		
15. Are complaints systematically registered and analyzed in your organization?		
16. Did you establish complaints handling procedures and are these routinely used in your organization?		
17. Do you measure the degree of customer loyalty?		
18. Do you make recommendations to customers about the products or services that best suit their needs?		
19. Do you know what the costs are when you lose a customer?		
20. Do you know what the costs are to gain a new customer?		
21. Do you know how much sales you lose due to unsatisfied customers?		
22. Do you regularly visit your customers?		
23. Do you regularly organize meetings with customer groups to learn about their needs, wants, ideas, and complaints?		
II Leadership	**Yes**	**No**
24. As a manager, do you know how many complaints are received yearly?		
25. Is there commitment at top-management for customer orientation?		
26. Did you integrate customer satisfaction into the norms and values of the organization?		
27. Are these norms and values clearly communicated to all your customers?		

Table 6.3 (Continued)

28. Does management recognize visible trends and do they anticipate these in a timely manner?		
29. Is management convinced of the importance of satisfied customers and do they act accordingly?		
30. Does management try to express the importance of satisfied customers to the organization at every occasion?		
31. Does management set a good example with regard to customer friendly behavior?		
32. Is management open to suggestions and ideas of customers?		
33. Does management personally reward those employees who deliver a valuable contribution to increased customers satisfaction?		
34. Are relationships with customers reasonably supported and stimulated by management?		
35. Is management at all times available to the customer?		
36. Does customer satisfaction also belong to the evaluation criteria of management?		
37. Are the customer wishes continuously taken into consideration when taking decisions?		
38. Does top management also personally handle complaints of customers?		
39. Do all members of management in the company have personal contact with external customers at least once a week?		
III Policy	Yes	No
40. Is customer satisfaction part of your organization's vision?		
41. Did you formulate concrete goals regarding the degree of customer satisfaction?		
42.Have you developed e-business strategies for the next two years to increase shareholder value?		
43. Is the customer satisfaction policy continuously communicated to all employees?		
44. Do you have a partnership relation with all your customers based on mutual respect and trust?		
45. Do you involve your customers in the development of promotional activities?		
46. Do you guarantee your customers a minimal service level and/or complete satisfaction?		
47. Is there continuous benchmarking with regard to customer satisfaction?		
48. Do you involve your customers with the execution of improvement processes in your company?		
49. Are more than 50% of your employees involved with the improvement of customer orientation?		
50. Do you have guidelines with regard to optimally satisfying the customer?		
51. Do you view customer information as a strategic asset?		
52. Do you have an up-to-date database in which all characteristics of your customers are registered?		

Table 6.3 (Continued)

IV Products/services and processes	Yes	No
53. Are products delivered within the period expected by the customer?		
54. Have you fully integrated the telephone, fax, Internet, and any other technology that the customer wants to use to do business?		
55. Is the phone in your organization answered within 3 rings in more than 90 % of the cases?		
56. Is every function and each process in your organization arranged to optimally comply with the expectations of your customers?		
57. Do these expectations form the basis for internal performance indicators?		
58. Are these indicators continuously measured and analyzed?		
59. Do you use measured customer satisfaction as an indicator for process improvement?		
60. Did you appoint process owners for controlling processes?		
61. Do you involve your customers in the development of new products and processes?		
62. Do you measure the satisfaction of your internal customers?		
63. Do supporting departments within your organization guarantee quality of the work they deliver?		
V Human Resource Management	**Yes**	**No**
64. Does customer orientation belong to the profile of the desired employee?		
65. Do you have an introduction program in which new employees are also educated concerning the importance of satisfied customers?		
66. Are your employees who continuously perform in a customer-oriented manner rewarded?		
67. Is training mandatory for each employee in your organization?		
68. Are customer orientation and continuous work towards improvement criteria for promotion?		
69. Do you regularly organize excursions for your employees to your important customers?		
70. Do your marketing employees receive a training of at least two weeks each year in customer orientation?		
71. Are your marketing employees free in taking decisions to satisfy customers?		
72. Are your marketing employees free to spend what is necessary to correct a mistake made with a customer?		
73. Do you involve your employees in improvement projects about increasing customer satisfaction?		
74. Do you stimulate your employees to generate ideas about increasing customer satisfaction?		
75. Are the employee's interest and the interest of the customer related?		

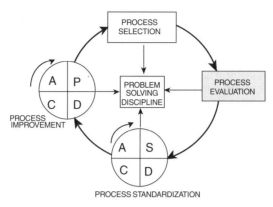

Figure 6.5 Step two in the quality improvement process

6.2 Process evaluation

In the second step of the QIP, *"process evaluation"*, the selected process is defined and consistently described and, based on measurements, checked whether the process is clearly understood and satisfies the needs of the customers (see figure 6.5). Measurements are used to: localize symptoms, verify causes, assess the need for process improvement, evaluate changes, ensure customer requirements have been met, provide standards for establishing comparisons, and give an indication of quality costs. Process performance is measured by making intensive use of the PSD tools. It is recommended to use flow-charts to display the process and related process steps. In this flow-chart, the locations (checkpoints) must be indicated where measurements should be taken to check and reduce process variation, in order to achieve a uniform quality. In this step, the improvement team will also be appointed and trained on the job in TQM. The possible causes and consequences of problems or bottlenecks are determined, as well as the most important performance indicators such as quality, time, and quantity.

Performance indicators

Processes are mostly measured on quality, throughput time, productivity, and added value. The throughput time of a process is the summary of the time that is spent executing the work and the waiting periods within the process. Productivity is the output and input ratio of a process, or the ratio between result and costs (Rampersad, 1995, 1996). Effectiveness and efficiency also say something about productivity. Effectiveness indicates the degree to which the objectives are realized and is also strongly related to quality. The output is central here. It's about *"doing the right things"*. Efficiency is closely related to the control of the process and the use of resources during the process execution. Here, the emphasis is on the input and the process whereas efficiency is about *"doing the things right"*. The general rule is: The shorter the throughput time, the more efficient the organiza-

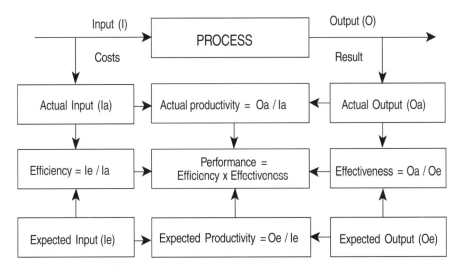

Figure 6.6 Concept table

tion. The concept table in figure 6.6 shows the relationship between these performance indicators. A distinction is also made between actual productivity, expected productivity and performance (In 't Veld, 1988). The concept of added value is increasingly used (on the output side) to judge the performance of processes. This indicator, which is also related to productivity, encompasses the difference between sales price of a product and the costs of raw material, goods and services to manufacture this product. In other words, it is the amount of value that is created with the output minus the value of the required input. Table 6.4 displays some important indicators to measure processes with the four mentioned criteria. Regarding the different productivity ratio's, a reference is made to Craig & Harris (1972).

Table 6.4 Performance indicators

Criteria	Indicators

Quality	– quality grade = {(production quantity - number of defects) / production quantity}x 100%
	 – failure rate = (number of failures / total number of products tested) x 100 %
	 – failure rate = (number of failures / operating time) x 100 %
	 – % rejects
	 – % scrap
	 – % communication failures
	 – number of suggestions per employee
	 – number of suggestions implemented
	 – usable strategic information as a % of available information
	 – % damaged
	 – % returns by customers
	 – % of processes which are statistically controlled
	 – % safety incidents
	 – % environmental incidents
	 – number of customer's complaints
	 – number of warranty claims
	 – delivery reliability; % delivery completed, on time, and according to the specifications
	 – % of processes with real-time quality feedback
	 – quality costs consisting of:
	    1. *Internal failure costs;* costs linked to correcting mistakes before delivery of the product, such as: scrap, rejects, adjustments, downtime of equipment, labor sitting idle while waiting for repairs, and sales discounts for inferior products,
	    2. *External failure costs;* costs which regard the adjustments of malfunctions after delivery of the product, such as: repair costs, travel and lodging expenses, replacement costs, stock spare parts, lost goodwill of customer, quarantee & warranty costs, and dispatchment costs.
	    3. *Prevention costs;* costs which are related to occurrence of the above mentioned costs such as: designing the product and the related process for quality, planning the quality control process, preventive maintenance costs, capital costs, quality training, and standard working procedures
	    4. *Judgement costs;* costs which have to do with measuring and evaluating products and processes to guarantee that these meet certain standards such as: input check, laboratory tests, acquiring special testing equipment, receiving inspection, reporting on quality, and ISO-audits.

Throughput time	– throughput time = processing time + inspection time + movement time + waiting time
	 – manufacturing cycle effectiveness = processing time / throughput time
	 – down time
	 – number of breakdowns
	 – availability = MTBF / MTTR
	    MTBF = Mean Time Between Failures
	    MTTR = Mean Time To Repair
	 – actual processing times vs. waiting times

Table 6.4 (Continued)

	- machine availability = {(production time – stoppage time) / production time} x 100 % - throughput time of failures = dispatch time – notice time - invoicing speed - time between order and delivery - time needed to present an offer - % of delayed orders - response time to a service request - lead time for product development - time needed to launch a new product on the market (time to market)
Productivity	- productivity = output / input = result / costs - actual productivity = actual result / actual costs - expected productivity = expected result / expected costs - result = output = (all produced units x sales price) + dividends - labor productivity = result / labor costs - labor costs = man hours x hourly wage - capital productivity = result / capital costs - capital costs = annuity value of used capital goods - material productivity = result / material costs - material costs = purchased material – storage costs - miscellaneous productivity = result / miscellaneous costs - miscellaneous costs = energy, maintenance, insurance, etc - integral productivity = result / (labor costs + capital costs + material costs + miscellaneous costs) - effectiveness = actual result / expected result - efficiency = expected costs / actual costs - revenue growth - market growth - sales growth - % of sales from new products - % absence due to illness - % personnel turnover - % of personnel who find that they are working under good management - % of personnel who find that they have challenging work - training costs as a percentage of sales - operational costs as a percentage of sales - return on investment - % of personnel with personal mission/vision linked to organizational mission/vision - profitability = (sales / costs) + interests received
Added value	- gross added value = sales - used raw material, goods and services needed to produce these products - net added value = gross added value – depreciation (consumption of durable capital goods) - added value per annual sales - added value per labor costs - added value per number of employees - added value per labor time - revenue per employee - purchase share as % of sales - circulation velocity of stock

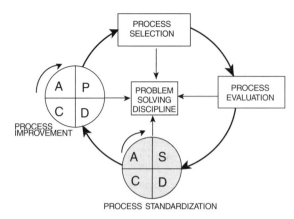

Figure 6.7 Step three in the quality improvement process

6.3 Process standardization

In the third step of the Quality Improvement Process, *"process standardization"*, the critical process which was described with a flow chart in the previous step, will be transformed into standard procedures so that each time the process can be executed in the same way (see figure 6.7). Process standardization is a means of defining a process and ensuring that everyone understands and employs it in a consistent manner. It entails the documentation of the current best-known way of performing a process, which provides the fundation from which to continuously improve the process. The working method is hereby documented in details to prevent employees from repeating old habits.

Clear procedures are drafted which include the process as well as relevant standards. The standards are based on measurements and related to customer's needs. For this, relevant check limits are determined for each measurement, based on feed-back from the customer and process capacity. In this way, the process performance can be registered and eventually adjusted.

While standardizing the present process, follow the *SDCA cycle (Standardize - Do - Check - Act)*:

- *Standardize.* Put the process in standard procedures on paper, communicate these procedures to the employees, and promote the procedures within the organization. People who participate in the process should develop the process standards.
- *Do.* Train employees in using these procedures, make them available, and urgently require the use of them.
- *Check.* Measure process performance according to the procedures and react to findings, identify the basic causes of process instability, and check if all the necessary means are available.
- *Act.* Judge and reduce the causes of process variability, document improvements, adjust procedures and document the lessons learned in this step.

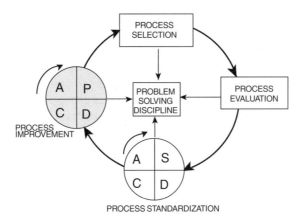

Figure 6.8 Step four in the quality improvement process

Before going on to the next step of improving the standardized process, it is important to consider the conditions for effective process execution, such as: improving the working environment, streamlining of process, use of maintenance systems, and adequate information gathering. This will benefit the effectiveness of process improvement.

6.4 Process improvement

In the fourth step of the quality improvement process, *"process improvement"*, the process is continuously being improved (see figure 6.8). In this phase, the registration of process performance also takes place and the standardization of improved processes is completed once again.

After the process is standardized, regular control of the effectiveness and stability of the process should be completed followed by eventual process improvement. To do this, the PDCA-cycle of Deming (Plan, Do, Check, Act) is used:

- **Plan.** Select, identify and define the problem, develop a questionnaire, gather the necessary information, analyze the available process data, determine the critical success factors, define performance indicators, determine the improvement goals, generate possible solutions for the problem, select a solution (also based on costs/benefits) and formulate an action plan to be able to implement the solution. Although a lot of these preparatory activities were already done during the first two steps, it is good to reconsider them in this step.
- *Do.* First execute the plan or solution on a limited scale, test the chosen solution and complete experiments if necessary. Describe the process which should be improved, complete cause and effect analyses, and identify the root causes. Train the team members in using quality improvement methods and techniques (see § 3.2).

- *Check.* Evaluate the results, which provide the solution with the help of the performance indicators, check whether the goals are realized and compare the results with the norm or theory. Start again if necessary.
- *Act.* Implement the solution or introduce the proven improvements, bring the process under control with the help of the "problem solving discipline", judge the results, document the lessons learned in this phase, improve and monitor the process continuously, and standardize the process adjustments. This assumes that the existing written working procedures should be changed or replaced, and that all employees should be informed about this. Make the new process standards available to everyone involved in the process as soon as possible, so all may begin to benefit from the latest improvements. Provide training to ensure that the standards are correctly implemented.

Because the SDCA and the PDCA cycle are continuously used, the process variability is continuously declining and the results are continuously improving. Continuous feedback from the customers is necessary in this phase to continue satisfying his/her needs. The step *"process selection"* in the quality improvement process should therefore continuously be used to keep up-to-date with the changing customer's needs, and to select the next critical process for improvement. This is illustrated in the QIP-model (see figure 6.8), by the line that goes to the starting point. As a result, the customer is continuously being satisfied. The six steps in the Problem Solving Discipline (see chapter 3) thus correspond with step 4 in this quality improvement process. So, the PSD is an integral part of this process.

Finally, it is recommended to evaluate teamwork and project results after completion of the project, indicate follow-up activities, document what was learned, show appreciation to the team members for their TQM efforts and eventually certify the improved process. Next, a new process is selected for improvement. The phasing of the quality improvement process is discussed further in chapter 9.

7 The TQM-organization

The way TQM is implemented differs for each organization and is mainly determined by the company size. In all cases, an integral and project-matic approach is
needed and commitment at the top management level. Top management must
formulate clear goals, continuously want to improve, completely support the introduction of TQM, participate actively in the related activities and coach, guide,
and support the implementation. Top management leads the improvement process, but each individual must also commit to and participate in the effort. Three
possible TQM-organization forms will be discussed in this chapter.

Organization form 1

Figure 7.1 shows a frequently occurring organization form consisting of:

- A TQM steering group.
- A TQM manager.
- TQM project teams or quality circles.

TQM steering group

The TQM steering group has the following composition:

- Chairperson: director
- Secretary: TQM manager
- Members: other members of the management team, department managers
                 (middle management), and an external TQM advisor

The TQM steering group has two important functions, namely:

1. Initiating, steering, supporting and promoting TQM activities, as well as creating the necessary conditions.

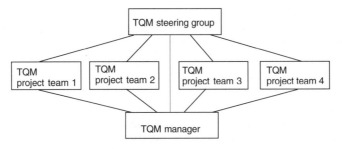

Figure 7.1 TQM organization form 1

2. Sponsorship. A sponsor is the person in the steering group who is supportive of the TQM project and always speaks in favor of the project. He/she is aware of the importance of the project. Therefore, he/she supports the project team, keeps the steering group informed about the project progress, provides support during implementation of the project results and functions as process owner. The process owner is responsible for the correct functioning of the process, is authorized to change that process, coordinates the process analyses and helps to put together the necessary project teams.

In large organizations, several steering groups are usually appointed (one steering group for each business unit), which are coordinated by one overall steering group. The TQM steering group meets once each month for one hour during regular working hours to discuss the progress of the TQM projects. The most important tasks of the TQM steering group are:

- formulating the project goals and related strategies;
- selecting the project or process which is eligible for improvement;
- phasing of the project, determining the milestones and time planning;
- selecting the team leaders;
- formulating tasks for the TQM project teams and functioning as a sponsor;
- determining the progress of the team activities;
- creating the basis for TQM in the organization;
- initiating TQM training activities;
- creating conditions for optimal functioning of the teams;
- supporting and coordinating project teams and promoting project implementation;
- reporting to top-management;
- advising top-management about TQM policy matters;
- testing the progress of TQM implementation within the organization.

TQM manager

The TQM manager is an expert in TQM and in charge of supporting the steering group, giving TQM training, and providing equipment to the TQM project teams and/or the quality circles.

TQM project team

A TQM project team is a group of experienced and knowledgeable employees from different disciplines put together by management to systematically address and solve certain complex problems. This team is temporarily appointed and consists of a team leader, a TQM facilitator, and other team members. The team leader leads the team, consults with the sponsor, carries out project activities, maintains contacts with the TQM steering group, and regularly organizes meetings. These meeting are held on a fixed day, time and place for one to one and a half hours (during normal working hours), starting twice a week and later on, once every two weeks. The teamleader is selected by the steering group based on his knowledge, experience, and leadership skills. The concerned sponsor (process owner) in the steering group forms the project team together with the team leader. The structure of the team depends on the problem definition. Usually, a team consists of 5 to 8 employees from different disciplines, who are knowledgeable and experienced in the distressed area, socially skilled and have a positive attitude towards the problem to be solved. The TQM facilitator coaches the team members, stimulates teamwork in the group, functions as an oracle for TQM, fulfils the function of process keeper, advises the team about the use of quality improvement techniques and methods, and monitors the project results. The tasks of the project teams are, among other things, brainstorming about the formulation of the problem, description of the process, process analyses, process improvement, adjustments of procedures, as well as documentation and reporting on project execution. Prior to the activities of the team, the TQM manager gives a short start-up course to the team members during which an explanation is given with respect to the TQM approach.

Quality circle

In addition to the efforts of project teams, quality circles are increasingly being used. The choice between project teams and quality circles depends on a large extend on the complexity of the problem, the company culture, and the organization structure. A quality circle, also called Kaizen team, is a group of volunteers who, during the normal working hours (a couple of hours per week) under supervision of their chief or trained facilitator, regularly identify and analyze all kinds of problems (which are not too complex, and which are related to their own work), and make recommendations to management regarding potential solutions to the problems. The group also works on implementing the solutions on the job. The quality control tools discussed in chapter three of this book are extensively used in this process. The premise of this Japanese concept is that the employees know the problems in their own work best, since they are the ones who face them every day. It is a form of participative management that encourages employee involvement and improves employee-management communication. A quality circle normally consists of a team of six to ten employees from the same department. In some organizations, quality circles consist not only of shop workers, but also of members of the management team, clerks, and persons involved from other disciplines.

Organization form 2

A second possible manner in which the TQM implementation can be organized is illustrated in figure 7.2 (Oakland, 1995). In this approach, the following hierarchical levels can be identified:

- A TQM steering group (see organization form 1).

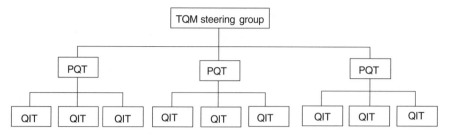

Figure 7.2 TQM organization form 2

- Process Quality Teams (PQTs) who function as process owners, and coordinate and guide improvement of critical processes ordered by the TQM steering group.
- Quality Improvement Teams (QITs) or quality circles who occupy themselves with detailed improvement of the critical processes.

The most important tasks of the PQT are:

- Describing critical processes indicated by the TQM steering group.
- Selecting critical processes which are eligible for improvement based on priorities.
- Guiding, coordinating, and supporting one or more QITs.
- Putting together QITs.
- Formulating tasks for the QITs.
- Determining the progress of the QIT activities.
- Preparing written reports for the TQM steering group.

The most important tasks of the QIT are:

- Mapping the appointed critical process by means of flow charts.
- Analyzing and measuring processes.
- Determining improvement actions to be taken.
- Executing improvement actions.
- Adjusting working procedures and documentation of the improvement process.
- Preparing written reports for the PQT.

The different teams are vertically and horizontally linked to each other in order to maintain consistency about the mission, vision, and goals on one hand, and to stimulate the learning process in the organization on the other. This is being realized by the role that the TQM-steering group and TQM-manager fulfill and by letting certain team members also actively participate in other teams.

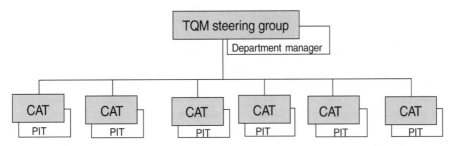

Figure 7.3 TQM organization form 3

Organization form 3

Figure 7.3 shows a third possible manner in which the TQM implementation can be organized. It consists of:
- A TQM steering group (see organization form 1).
- Corrective Action Teams (CATs) who analyze processes and than correct them in order to control the process. The CAT is temporarily appointed by the TQM steering group and receives the assignment from this group.
- Process Improvement Teams (PITs) structurally improve and maintain the corrected processes, and secure the TQM working method. Thus, after the CAT makes the process controllable, it will continuously be improved and maintained by the PIT to prevent losing the results of the CAT after implementation. The PIT is permanently appointed by the department manager and receives orders from him.

This organization form is central in the implementation of Statistical Process Control (see also Does, 1996). A CAT is made up of 5 to 8 employees who are closely involved in the daily routine of their process, such as executors and operators. A representative of the different supporting departments is usually also added to the team, such as a maintenance serviceman and a quality control official. The CAT leader functions as the chairperson and is someone from the concerned department. The most important tasks of the CAT are:

- Mapping and describing the concerned process.
- Conducting process analyses and measurements. Tracking causes of mistakes and consequences, and arranging them according to priority.
- Defining improvement actions.
- Taking measures to secure process control.
- Adjusting working procedures.
- Buying or making work aids.
- Completing written reports for the steering group.

The tasks of the CAT and the TQM steering groups are in accordance with the first three steps in the quality improvement process *("process selection", "process eval-*

uation", and *"process standardization").* This is shown in figure 6.2. The CAT receives the order from the TQM steering group, which contains the result to be obtained (objective), when this should be realized, reporting frequently to the steering group, and what is expected of everyone. When the order is accomplished, the TQM steering group dissolves the CAT, after acknowledging the results and determining any eventual reward. The steering group (in collaboration with an experienced auditor), usually closes this stage by testing the results and certifying the process. This is done, to determine whether an implemented TQM working method and controlled process exists in the work place. If this is satisfied, the CAT receives a certificate that is valid for one year. After this period, the process should be certified once again. This does not mean that they are finished and can relax. After the CAT makes the process controllable, it should be continuously improved and maintained in order to prevent the obtained results from disappearing subsequent to implementation. To achieve this, a Process Improvement Team (PIT) is appointed. The CAT than changes into a PIT.

The composition of a PIT corresponds to that of a CAT, but it can eventually consist of the same members. Here, it also includes employees who are closely involved with the daily activities of their own process, supplemented by involved employees from other disciplines who regularly meet on a fixed day, time and place. Just as with the CAT, the PIT also has a chairperson and a secretary. On this level, the PIT is not appointed by the TQM steering group but by the department manager. The PIT receives the order from him. In this case, the department manager functions as the steering group. The PIT has accomplished its goal if improvement actions are executed continuously according to facts. The tasks of the PIT are among other things:

- Registering, arranging, and counting (with a check sheet) all process failures in a logbook.
- Completing process analyses and measurements.
- Determining the priority per process failure and documenting the improvement actions taken (with the help of the FMEA-technique).
- Executing improvement actions; also improving security, tidiness and ergonomics, decreasing scrap, etc.
- Adjusting the working procedures.
- Continuously documenting the improvement process.
- Completing written reports for all department managers (at least every two weeks).

The most important tasks of the department manager are:

- Documenting the goals and related strategies.
- Phasing the approach, determining the milestones, and time planning.
- Putting together the PITs.
- Formulating the orders for the PITs.
- Determining the progress of PIT activities.
- Initiating training.

- Creating conditions for optimal functioning of the PITs.
- Guiding and coordinating the PITs.

The tasks of the PIT and the department manager are in accordance with the PDCA-cycle for continuous improvement; the step "process improvement" in the quality improvement process (see figure 6.2). This implies that the PIT will not be dissolved. The composition may eventually be changed.

8 Managing change

8.1 Resistance against change

TQM regards change, which is inevitable and essential for the growth of an organization. Unfortunately, most people within an organization despise and resist change. They are afraid of change and resist it by nature, because it affects their established ideas and opinions. Disappointments from previous experiences with activities, involving change, may account for this. In view of this, two kinds of people can be distinguished in an organization:

1. people who think that they will be the victim of change and therefore resist, become angry and depressed;
2. people who support change completely, design and plan for the change.

Especially in the initial phase of the project implementation, resistance seems to be very high because certain people within the organization see this as a threat due to the related uncertainties and obscurity. Other reasons for people to resist are: the need for additional information, deep mistrust, and lack of understanding. Because of this, conflicts emerge whereby people frequently refer to the old reliable situation. Examples of expressing resistance are:

- Let us stay with both feet on the ground.
- I don't see why we must change, everything is going good as it is.
- We are the best in the market.
- In our organization it is absolutely not possible.
- We have always done it well this way.
- At the moment, we are too busy for that.
- That costs too much.
- We have tried that already and it didn't work.
- It is against our principles.
- We are too small for that.
- I'm certain it is not going to work.
- If it isn't broken, then don't fix it.

According to James O' Toole (1996), there are lots of reasons for people to resist change. These are described in the adjoining frame.

James O'Toole's thirty-three hypotheses for why people resist change

1. Homeostasis – change is not a natural condition.
2. Stare decisis – presumption given to the status quo; burden of proof is on change.
3. Inertia – takes considerable power to change course.
4. Satisfaction – most people like the way things are.
5. Lack of ripeness – the preconditions for change haven't been met; the time isn't right.
6. Fear – people fear the unknown.
7. Self-interest - the change may be good for others but not us.
8. Lack of self-confidence – we don't think we are up to the new challenges.
9. Future shock – overwhelmed by change, we hunker down and resist it.
10. Futility – we view all change as superficial, cosmetic, and illusory, so why bother?
11. Lack of knowledge – we don't know how to change or what to change to.
12. Human nature – humans are competitive, aggressive, greedy, and selfish and lack the altruism necessary to change.
13. Cynicism – we suspect the motives of the change agent.
14. Perversity – change sounds good but we fear that the unintended consequences will be bad.
15. Individual genius versus group mediocrity – those of us with mediocre minds can't see the wisdom of the change.
16. Ego – the powerful refuse to admit that they have been wrong.
17. Short-term thinking – people can't defer gratification.
18. Myopia – we can't see that the change is in the broader self-interest.
19. Sleepwalking – most of us lead unexamined lives.
20. Snow blindness – groupthink, or social conformity.
21. Collective fantasy – we don't learn from experience and view everything in the light of preconceived notions.
22. Chauvinistic conditioning – we are right; they who want us to change are wrong.
23. Fallacy of the exception – the change might work elsewhere but we are different.
24. Ideology – we have different worldviews – inherently conflicting values.
25. Institutionalism – individuals may change but groups do not.
26. "Natura no facit saltum" – "nature does not proceed by leaps"
27. The rectitude of the powerful – who are we to question the leaders who set us on the current course?
28. "Change has no constituency" – the minority has a greater stake in preserving the status quo than the majority has in changing.
29. Determinism – there is nothing anyone can do to bring about purposeful change.
30. Scientism – the lessons of history are scientific and therefore there is nothing to learn from them
31. Habit.
32. The despotism of custom – the ideas of change agents are seen as a reproach to society.
33. Human mindlessness.

Source: James O'Toole, Leading Change: The Argument for Values-Based Leadership, Ballantine Books, New York, 1999, pp. 161-164

These resistance reactions can frustrate the process of change completely, if there is no adequate reaction to this. These negative reactions are divided in the following phases:

1. *Passiveness.* They are informed about the new plans which is accompanied by a reaction of uncertainty.
2. *Denial.* They are skeptical and deny the exactness of the suggested improvement plans.

3. *Anger.* If the plans continue, they react angrily and quit.
4. *Negotiation.* They try to reach a compromise (through negotiations) by minimizing the proposals and partially accepting the plans.
5. *Depression.* Because the complete proposal must be implemented, they'll have to accept the change. This results in passive behavior, which eventually ends in depression.
6. *Acceptance.*

These different phases must be acknowledged immediately and proper measures taken. During the passive and depression phase, an understanding attitude of the manager is required to be open to the mentioned reactions. During the phase of denial, anger and negotiation, a firm attitude of the manager is required. The different phases of the employees must be recognized early and should be brought as soon as possible into the phase of acceptance. That is why those who completely accept the change should be involved in improvement projects.

Methods to handle resistance are:

- Top management must communicate face-to-face and give information about the what, why, and how of change. John Kotter (1998) explains that before most people can understand and accept a proposed change they seek answers to a lot of questions, such as (see also Boyett, 1998):

- What will this mean to me?
- What will it mean to my friends?
- What will it mean to the organization?
- What other alternatives are there?
- Are there better options?
- If I'm going to operate differently, can I do it?
- How will I learn the new skills I will need?
- Will I have to make sacrifices? What will they be? How do I feel about having to make them?
- Do I really believe this change is necessary?
- Do I really believe what I'm hearing about the direction for the future?
- Is this the right direction for us to take?
- Are others playing some game, perhaps to improve their position at my expense?

- Be honest about the actual situation. State clearly how long the change will last and what the consequences will be on the quality of labor. Provide information on time. Silence creates doubt and usually causes rumors to spread, which undermines their trust in management. Don't provide too much information at once, because employees need time to absorb the information.
- Support the proposals with clear arguments;
- Inform the employees about the advantages of change and how the gap between future and present situations must be closed;
- Have meetings with those who show clear resistance and give a detailed reaction to all their objections;
- Involve concerned employees in the project;

- Involve key persons and the union in the decision making process. After all, if the stakeholders are involved in decision making, acceptation will be much bigger and therefore, also the effect. Involve also change agents to facilitate, monitor and encourage change.
- Put the project on hold if there is too much resistance and you're not able to count on the support of the majority.

There are also other methods to motivate change and stimulate active participation, such as:

1. Probe continuously if they are ready to change.
2. Communicate with employees in a series of meetings about the formulated mission, vision, core values, goals, and strategies of the organization. Show employees why we are changing and how their lives will be better. This concept should be evangelized and communicated internally and externally, both verbally and in writing. Keep it simple and use analogies, examples, and many different forums. The use of brochures, bulletin boards and newsletters is recommended. Williams Pasmore (1994) states that much of your communication effort may involve educating your employees about the business and the competitive environment, such as the ones listed in the following frame.

What employees need to know about their company

- Employees need to know what managers know, including how to read the income statement and the balance sheet, what makes the number on each get larger or smaller, what the numbers really mean, and were the company stands today compared to where it's been historically and versus the competition.
- Employees need to know the treats to the organization and the plans to deal with them, including an understanding of why the plans make sense and what other alternatives were considered before deciding on this course of action.
- Employees need to understand decision-making processes and criteria and how much risk is acceptable.
- Employees need to understand the consequences of making poor decisions and what to do when the unexpected happens.
- Employees need to understand customers' expectations and how to better meet them.
- Employees need to be introduced to global economics.
- Employees need to know about health-care costs and about workers' compensation, about the costs of carrying inventory and liability insurance.
- Employees need to understand the technical system used to produce goods or services how it functions and why it was designed as it was designed.
- Employees need to understand what technical alternatives are possible and what would be involved in applying them.
- Employees need to develop the social skills that allow them to take part in participative activities, including speaking up in front of others, confronting differences, understanding how to reach consensus, facilitating the participation of others, and listening.

Source: William Pasmore, Creating Strategic Change: Designing the Flexible High-Performing Organization, John Wiley & Sons, New York, 1994, p.p. 50-54.

3. Indicate why there is a need to change. The organization must be convinced of the necessity for change. A popular way to do this is by comparing the organization with more successful competitors (benchmarking), analyzing the dissatisfaction of customers, and illustrating the continuously decreasing performance indicators. Make it clear that in the long run under extreme conditions, survival of the organization will be at stake. The present situation must be seen as negative. They have to realize that the current situation is not satisfactory. By doing this, skeptics can be convinced of the necessity to change. By making people acknowledge that the organization is doing poorly, dissatisfaction with the present situation is created. Robert Jacobs (1994) introduces the following formula to establish a need to change:

$$C = A \times B \times D > X$$

Where:

C = the probability of change being successful
A = dissatisfaction with the status quo
B = a clear statement of the desired end state after the change
D = concrete first steps toward the goal
X = the cost of change

The formula states that if you want people to change you have to (A) convince them that they need to change, (B) provide a vision of how much better their lives will be if they do change, and (D) demonstrate that you know what you are doing by generating some positive results early in the change process.

John Kotter (1996) thinks that bold actions must be taken to convince employees of a needed change, such as the ones listed in the adjoining frame.

Bold Ways to Convince Employees of a Needed Change

According to Kotter, being bold means doing such things as:

- Cleaning up the balance sheet and creating a huge loss for the quarter
- Selling corporate headquarters and moving into a building that looks like a battle command center
- Telling all your businesses that they have 24 months to become first or second in their Markets, with the penalty for failure being divestiture or closure
- Making 50% of the top pay for the top 10 officers based on tough product-quality targets for the whole organization
- Exposing managers to a major weakness vis à vis competitors
- Allowing errors to blow up instead of being corrected at the last minute
- Eliminating obvious examples of excess (e.g. company-owned country-club facilities, a large air force, gourmet executive dining rooms)
- Insisting that more people at lower levels be held accountable for broad measure of business performance
- Sending more data about customer satisfaction and financial performance to more employees, especially information that demonstrates weaknesses vis-à-vis the competition
- Insisting people talk regularly to unsatisfied customers, unhappy suppliers, and disgruntled shareholders
- Putting more honest discussions of the firm's problems in company newspapers and senior management speeches.

Source: John P. Kotter, Leading Change, Harvard Business School Press, Boston, 1996, p. 44.

4. Base the improvement proposals on solid grounds. A distinct solution must be presented.
5. Illustrate clearly how the change will be implemented. Based on a solid implementation plan in which the steps to be taken are explained. During the process of change, provide the employees regularly with trustworthy information to keep them informed.
6. Introduce training sessions to develop skills of the employees such as TQM, e-business, client orientation, teamwork, leadership, etc.
7. Involve concerned employees in planning and the introduction of change; involvement of people is of essential importance for the successful introduction of change. Without continuous involvement of the relevant employees, every project is doomed to fail.
8. Reward those who produce results; use intrinsic rewards (such as pride, praise, and recognition) in preference to extrinsic rewards (such as money). Each success must get a lot of attention. Give credit to all groups and individuals who contribute to success and minimize your own importance. Those who produce results, no matter how small, must be seen as a hero. In addition, those who stagnate and oppose must either be encouraged to change their attitude, be moved to another location in the organization, or dismissed. Be prepared to take these measures, because one rotten apple in the organization can completely disturb and frustrate the process of change.
9. Provide the reorganization project with a strong identity. An ambitious name whereby employees feel they have a real goal (a dream) towards which to work together.
10. Start carefully; start with a pilot project and practice with it. Start with the easiest part of the project which can produce results. The scale of change must not exceed the capacity of individuals. Make choices based on business imperatives.
11. Create commitment at top management for continuous improvement. Top management must take the lead to achieve change. They should place TQM on the agenda of the management team meetings every month, manage stakeholders, build project and work group teams, transfer knowledge, and communicate change.
12. Start the continuous improvement process at the highest level and cascade it through the organization, layer by layer.
13. Eliminate those elements which demoralize and de-motivate individuals in the organization.
14. Give leaders and teams the authority and ownership over the processes for which they are responsible.
15. Make the employees shareholders, so they will behave as owners.
16. Provide an objective review and a fitting rewarding, educational, talent development, and severance system.

Before applying change, it will be necessary to verify if the circumstances are favorable for implementation. Insight into the expected problems during the execution will be needed. Table 8.1 shows a checklist, which can be used to gain insight in the implementation circumstances of the transformation project. The implementation circumstances are unfavorable if there are too many questions that were answered with "no". These questions should then receive extra attention.

Table 8.1 Checklist implementation circumstances

	Yes	Slightly	No
1. Commitment			
• Is there commitment at top management for change?	O	O	O
• Are the proposed changes experienced by those involved crucial for the survival?	O	O	O
• Is attention paid to the involvement of all key persons in the decision making?	O	O	O
2. Ability			
• Are the skills of the change manager in accordance with the execution demands?	O	O	O
• Are the personnel and material conditions adequate for change?	O	O	O
• Is attention being paid to the development of new skills of the personnel?	O	O	O
3. Values			
• Is the change in accordance with the social and ethical values of those involved?	O	O	O
• Is the change in accordance with the philosophy and policy of the organization?	O	O	O
• Are the core values of the organization closely related to the goals of change?	O	O	O
4. Information & communication			
• Is the information about the change clear?	O	O	O
• Can the idea behind the change be made understandable for everyone?	O	O	O
• Is there adequate information available about the what, why, how and causes of change?	O	O	O
• Is the necessity for change communicated to those involved?	O	O	O
• Are the improvement proposals based on solid facts?	O	O	O
• Is there a clear implementation plan in which the steps to be taken are clearly explained?	O	O	O
• Are the change objectives defined?	O	O	O
5. Timing			
• Is this the right moment for the introduction of change?	O	O	O
• Are there other events in the organization which will decrease the chances of success if the change is implemented?	O	O	O
6. Necessity			
• Is the need large enough to introduce change?	O	O	O
• Are the benefits of change well balanced?	O	O	O
7. Resistance			
• Is attention being paid to those who will not benefit from this change?	O	O	O
• Are all causes of previously arisen resistance carefully analyzed and solved?	O	O	O
• Is there little resistance against change?	O	O	O
• Do the majority of the employees support change?	O	O	O

In summary, it can be stated that:

> *no need + no awareness + no opportunities + no communication +*
> *no involvement + no commitment = no change*

8.2 Cultural change

Experience has shown that introduction of Total Quality Management is closely related to change and the necessary apportionment of the organizational culture. The organizational culture encompasses the common behavior of all employees in the organization with regard to their work, the organization and their relations with customers, suppliers, and colleagues. The organizational culture can also be described as a consolidation of opinions, ideas, values, rules, behavioral patterns, and norms of the people within the organization. The organizational culture is expressed in for instance: the nature of the people (good, bad, passive, customer oriented, respect for the individual, focussed on performance, etc.), the nature of their personal relations (teamwork, solidarity, effort, competition), style of management (dominant, human-oriented), formal statements (such as mission, and vision), organizational structure (bureaucratic, self-supporting autonomous units), HRM-policy (reviewing, rewarding, training), communication system (formal, informal, open), specific rules (conduct rules, guide lines, procedures), and the specific traditions of the organization. Edgar Schein (1990) demonstrates how an organization can develop its own culture through the following frame on the next page.

Successful introduction of TQM requires cultural change, which above all things requires the fundamental adjustment of the behavior of people in the organization (Peters & Waterman, 1982). This behavior is strongly related to principles, namely what is considered normal or decent in the organization. These principles are translated into the values and norms of the organization. The values are the feelings about that which is commonly pursued and considered important. Norms are related to the written and unwritten rules, which indicate the behavior that is expected of someone. Effective leadership (see § 5.5) is one of the most important cultural change techniques. Thus, a leader must coach in such a way that the people want to change instead of having the feeling that they have to change. First, the leader will have to start changing him and set a good example, such as fulfilling his appointments on time, no expensive company car, and no high expense account. When cutting wages, the leader must start cutting his salary. If he wants to improve internal communication in his organization, he must start with himself by listening to others instead of only talking. If he wants to improve the quality of the employees through training, he must set an example by going to a training first. If the leader wants to be trusted, he must be trustworthy.

Developing an Organization Culture

Culture can be thought of as the way an organization's members, and particularly its founders, have resolved important issues, such as:

- *The organization's relationship to its environment*
  Does the organization perceive itself to be dominant, submissive, harmonizing, or searching for a niche?

- *The nature of human activity*
  Is the correct way for humans to behave to be dominant/proactive, harmonizing, or passive/fatalistic?

- *The nature of reality and truth*
  How do we define what is true and what is not?
  How is truth ultimately determined both in the physical and social world-by pragmatic test, reliance on wisdom, or social consensus?

- *The nature of time*
  What is our basic orientation in terms of past, present, and future?
  What kinds of time units are most relevant for the conduct of daily affairs?

- *The nature of human nature*
  Are humans basically good, neutral, or evil?
  Is human nature perfectible or fixed?

- *The nature of human relationships*
  What is the correct way for people to relate to each other to distribute power and affection?
  Is life competitive or cooperative?
  Is the best way to organize society on the basis of individualism or groupism?
  Is the best authority system autocratic/paternalistic or collegial/participative?

- *Homogeneity versus diversity*
  Is the group best off if it is highly diverse or if it is highly homogeneous?
  Should individuals in a group be encouraged to innovate or conform?

Source: Edgar Schein, "Organizational Culture", American Psychologist, February 1990, p. 114

Strong cultures are not only characterized by effective leadership but also by:

- Taking care of all stakeholders in a balanced way.
- High motivation, active participation, and devotion to realize the stated goals.
- A strong involvement of employees in the decision making process.
- Teamwork, mutual trust, respect, and a "we-feeling".
- Clear recognizable assumptions about the required behavior.
- The feeling by employees that their individual performance contributes to the realization of the organization's goals.
- A shared sense by everyone for what the organization as a whole is trying to accomplish.
- A sense of personal responsibility by everyone for the overall performance of the organization.
- Top-down, bottom-up, and horizontal (free and open) communication.
- Regular feedback to employees to learn new skills.

- Constantly searching and trying of new ideas.
- Employees and managers who are open to change and are convinced that this would lead to improvement.
- Multifunctional usability, flexibility, and willingness of the employees towards change.
- Environmental support of employees to perform the work. Thomas Gilbert (1987) identifies three environmental supports of employees: *information* (about objectives, what is expected of them, etc.), *instruments* (tools, techniques, procedures, etc.), and *incentives* (monetary and/or non-monetary). He states that if you take away some or all of the environmental supports or ignore the person's repertory of behavior, you will create incompetence (see the next frame).

Behavior model for creating incompetence

1. Withhold information.
   Don't let people know how well they are performing.
   Give people misleading information about how well they are performing.
   Hide from people what is expected from them.
   Give people little or no guidance about how to perform well.

2. Don't involve people in selecting the instruments of work.
   Design the tools of work without ever consulting the people who will use them.
   Keep the engineers away from the people who will use the tools.

3. Don't provide incentives for good performance.
   Make sure that poor performers get paid as well as good ones.
   See that good performance gets punished in some way.
   Don't make use of non-monetary incentives.

4. Don't help people improve their skills.
   Leave training to chance.
   Put training in the hands of supervisors who are not trained instructors.
   Make training unnecessarily difficult.
   Make training irrelevant to the employee's purposes.

5. Ignore the individual's capacity.
   Schedule performance for times when people are not at their sharpest.
   Select people for tasks they have intrinsic difficulties in performing.
   Do not provide response aids.

6. Ignore the individual's motives.
   Design the job so that it has no future.
   Avoid arranging working conditions that employees would find more pleasant.
   Give pep talks rather than incentives to promote performance in punishing situations.

Source: Thomas F. Gilbert. Human competence: Engineering worthy performance. McGraw-Hill, 1987.

Timothy Galpin (1996) identifies ten cultural components to consider when implementing change, as described in the following frame.

Ten cultural components to consider when implementing change

1. *Rules and Policies*
Eliminate rules and policies that will hinder performance of new methods and procedures. Create new rules and policies that reinforce desired ways of operating. Develop and document new standard operating procedures.

2. *Goals and Measurement*
Develop goals and measurements that reinforce desired changes. Make goals specific to operations. For example, establish procedural goals and measures for employees conducting the process that is to be changed, rather than financial goals that are a by-product of changing the process and that employees cannot easily relate to their actions.

3. *Customs and Norms*
Eliminate old customs and norms that reinforce the old ways of doing things and replace them with new customs and norms that reinforce the new ways. For example, replace written memos to convey information through the organization with face-to-face weekly meetings of managers and their teams.

4. *Training*
Eliminate training that reinforces the old way of operating and replace it with training that reinforces the new. Deliver training "just-in-time" so people can apply it immediately. Develop experiential training that provides real-time, hands-on experience with new processes and procedures.

5. *Ceremonies and Events*
Establish ceremonies and events that reinforce new ways of doing things, such as awards ceremonies and recognition events for teams and employees who achieve goals or successfully implement changes.

6. *Management Behaviors*
Develop goals and measurements that reinforce the desired behaviors. Provide training that focuses on the new behaviors. Publicly recognize and reward managers who change by linking promotion and pay rewards to the desired behaviors. Penalize managers who do not change behaviors. For example, do not give promotions or pay increases or bonuses to managers who do not demonstrate the desired behaviors.

7. *Rewards and Recognition*
Eliminate rewards and recognition that reinforce old methods and procedures, replace them with new rewards and recognition that reinforce the desired ways of operating. Make rewards specific to the change goals that have been set.

8. *Communications*
Eliminate communication that reinforces the old way of operating; replace it with communication that reinforces the new. Deliver communication in new ways to show commitment to change. Use multiple channels to deliver consistent messages before, during, and after changes are made. Make communications two-way by soliciting regular feedback from management and employees about the changes being made.

9. *Physical Environment*
Establish a physical environment that reinforces the change. Relocate management and employees who will need to work together to make changes successful. Use "virtual offices" to encourage people to work outside the office with customers and telecommunications to connect people who need to interact from a distance.

10. *Organizational Structure*
Establish an organizational structure that will reinforce operational changes. For example, set up client service teams, eliminate management layers, centralize or decentralize work as needed, combine overlapping divisions.

Source: Timothy Galpin, "Connecting Culture to Organizational Change", HRMagazine, March 1996, pp. 84-90.

8.3 Cultural typology according to Harrison

Harrison (1972) has developed a typology of organizational cultures to gain insight about the level of change mindedness of organizations. According to him, the organizational culture can be divided in four types:

1. Power-oriented culture
2. Role-oriented culture
3. Task-oriented culture
4. Personal-oriented culture

The characteristics of a *power-oriented culture* are:

- Association is determined by personal power (personality is central).
- Decision making based on power.
- Rules of the central man are important.
- Change can be quick and depends on the person.
- Strong people in key positions.
- Maintaining power first.
- Rivalry among the managers to obtain power and personal gain at the expense of their colleagues.

The characteristics of a *role-oriented culture* are:

- Association is determined by communication and behavior patterns (titles count).
- Decision making based on procedures and formal positions (subordination to rules).
- Reacts difficult to changed situations (slow formal decision making).
- Responsibilities are clearly defined and everyone stays within the area for which he/she is responsible.
- Bureaucracy (functional organization).
- Behavior in the organization is very predictable.

The characteristics of a *task-oriented culture* are:

- Association is determined by the tasks to be done (doing is central).
- Decision making based on what is needed at this instance for these tasks.
- Reacts promptly to changes.
- Results first (do first, think later).
- Authority is based on knowledge and capability to accomplish the tasks.
- Realization of goals is central, rules are unimportant.

The characteristics of a *personal-oriented culture* are:
- The needs of people are central.
- Limited management tasks.

- Decision making through consensus.
- Employees support each other.
- Internal orientation.

To create insight in your own organizational culture, Harrison recommends the following approach:

A) Answering certain culture related questions.
B) Classifying the answers according to the four typologies.
C) Displaying this in a diagram, in order to make the organizational culture explicit.

A) *Answering certain culture related questions.*

1. For each of the following questions, indicate how your department or organization is functioning, by writing in the column "present" a 1, 2, 3, or 4 (see table 8.2).
2. After you've answered all questions, repeat the list in the column "desired" from the angle of: "how do you want your organization to function".

Table 8.2 Culture related questions

No.	Question	Present	Desired
1	If someone in our organization has a difference of opinion with a colleague then: 1) A discussion starts whereby the best wins. 2) They will put the conflict before their chief who will make a decision. 3) Together they decide what is best for the organization and act accordingly. 4) They discuss it, after which each one does what he/she finds best.		
2	If the organization can gain from a certain situation, whereby risks must be taken and a few rules and procedures temporarily suspended, then: 1) We only do it if it can be reasonably done without neglecting the rules. 2) Everyone involved goes quickly to gather information to test the feasibility and if it is positive, we do it. 3) Usually, there is only interest from the entire group if they find it an interesting assignment. After all, no one will object to someone else doing the assignment. 4) Management decides and explains to everyone what to do.		
3	The reasons why people in our organization make an effort are mainly: 1) Because the assignment must be brought to a favorable end and we are all responsible for that. 2) Because we can only achieve something if we all work hard at it; moreover, we'll have to deal with the boss if we don't work at it. 3) Because the assignment has our attention and has become part of ourselves. 4) Because it is expected that we regularly keep working and deliver a good performance.		

Table 8.2 (Continued)

4	If someone in our organization has a quarrel with the chief, then: 1) Colleagues will talk to him or her and help solve the problem; but if that does not help they will stay at odds and avoid each other in the future (or the person involved will look for another job). 2) There is a regular procedure that can be followed by the person involved to get a binding decision. 3) He will try to dominate the chief, but will usually admit. 4) It's a question of whether it is important to the job; if not, then it is not interesting. If it is, then colleagues will see to it that the quarrel is settled.		
5	If someone in our organization is not satisfied with the assignment, he will usually: 1) Make a request for change or talk to the chief or personnel department. 2) Make another contribution within the job to be done. 3) Push for a promotion. 4) Do other work or look for another job.		
6	If by achieving a certain goal, someone in our organization must be deprived or be hurt, then: 1) Colleagues help such a person accept this; if they do not succeed, then it's a pity and he will leave. 2) The person in question will have to make the best of it. 3) It depends if it's a high or a low ranking official. It doesn't happen that easily with a high ranking and influential person; it usually happens to someone in a lower position. 4) It is traced how it was done in previous cases and if any compensation was given; depending on this, something might be done.		
7	If a competitor threatens to take away one of our jobs, then: 1) We check if he breaks any rules by doing this; if he does, then we will protest. If he doesn't, then there is little to do and the customer decides eventually. 2) It is annoying for him who has done his best; colleagues help him, but if he loses from the competitor, he will have to look for another nice assignment. 3) We wait and see for a while, then go all out to get the assignment. Sometimes we succeed by improving our approach; if not, then it is wise to concentrate on another task. 4) We try to be a step ahead of our competitor. Willingly or not, we'll have to beat them.		
8	If someone cannot keep up any longer, then: 1) He will entrench himself, try to find a strong position and fight back. 2) Usually, he will be transferred or pushed up by getting promoted. 3) Colleagues accept it and help the person involved accept it. 4) Someone else will get the assignment and the person involved will do something else if possible.		

Table 8.2 (Continued)

9	If suddenly a leading official falls out and has to be replaced, then: 1) Usually the assistant chief, who has been working there the longest or has the right papers and good evaluations, will be appointed. 2) Management will appoint someone who they find capable and competent. 3) Colleagues must choose someone who is skilled and capable as a leader and as a person, and who has the trust of the employees. 4) Look for someone who can cope with this position and manage to keep everything together.		
10	If there is a question of introducing a change in working conditions (e.g. other working hours), then: 1) It is being consulted; probably a committee is installed to suggest a proposal 2) It's the question of whether people will be better off by that. Those who feel that way will make use of it, whereas others don't have to. 3) It depends on what management finds; if he finds it damaging he will try to stop introduction or limit it; if he doesn't find it damaging, he will permit it (within reasonable boundaries); 4) We will determine what they contain and what the effects will be on the job. If the job permits it than change will be introduced, while the colleagues try to make arrangements among themselves to handle the problems.		

B) *Classifying the answers according to the four cultural typologies*
In table 8.3, cross the circle per question by each of the chosen possibilities, and give the total score at the bottom of the table per cultural typology (count the number of times you've scored A, B, C or D). For example, if the answer of question 1 is possibility 3, then you cross circle C.

Table 8.3 Classifying answers according to the four cultural typologies

Question	Possibility	Present Culture				Possibility	Desired Culture			
		A	B	C	D		A	B	C	D
1	1	O				1	O			
	2		O			2		O		
	3			O		3			O	
	4				O	4				O
2	1		O			1		O		
	2			O		2			O	
	3			O		3				O
	4	O				4	O			
3	1			O		1			O	
	2	O				2	O			
	3				O	3				O
	4		O			4	O			
4	1				O	1				O
	2		O			2		O		
	3	O				3	O			
	4			O		4			O	
5	1		O			1		O		
	2			O		2			O	
	3	O				3	O			
	4				O	4				O
6	1				O	1				O
	2			O		2			O	
	3	O				3	O			
	4		O			4		O		
7	1		O			1		O		
	2				O	2				O
	3			O		3			O	
	4	O				4	O			
8	1	O				1	O			
	2		O			2		O		
	3				O	3				O
	4			O		4			O	
9	1		O			1		O		
	2	O				2	O			
	3				O	3				O
	4			O		4			O	
10	1		O			1		O		
	2				O	2				O
	3	O				3	O			
	4			O		4			O	
Total										

A = power-oriented culture, B = role-oriented culture, C = task-oriented culture, D = personal-oriented culture

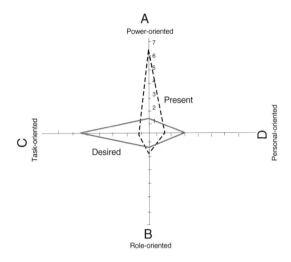

Figurr 8.1 Culture diagram

C) *Displaying answers in a culture diagram*

In table 8.4, fill in how many times you've scored A, B, C or D (separately for "present" and "desired"). By connecting the four points with a line, the mix of cultures for your organization is displayed. Give the two profiles a different color. Discuss the differences and resemblances. Figure 8.1 gives an example of a present power-oriented organizational culture and a desired task-oriented organizational culture. The most important recommendations per culture form are given in table 8.4.

Table 8.4 Recommendations per organization culture

Power-oriented	Seek contact with those in power
Role-oriented	Make sure that the working method is procedurally documented
Task-oriented	Make sure that the results of the job correspond with the organization's goals
Personal-oriented	Make sure that activities correspond with the interest of the employees

8.4 Culture diagnoses according to Hofstede

Hofstede (1991) has developed a cultural diagnostic system in order to gain insight into the different organizational cultures. He distinguishes the following six dimensions:

1. Process-oriented vs. result-oriented
2. Personal-oriented vs. job-oriented
3. Organizationally linked vs. professional
4. Open vs. closed
5. Tight control vs. easy control
6. Pragmatic vs. normative

These six dimensions are shown in table 8.5. Judge each dimension in your organization on a scale of 1 to 5. Discuss the results of this culture diagnosis and try to figure out why it is that these are typical for your organization. Make a plan to realize a cultural change.

Table 8.5 Culture diagnosis in six dimensions

1) PROCESS-ORIENTED	1	2	3	4	5	RESULT-ORIENTED
– Avoiding risks – Little exertion as possible – Every day the same						– At ease in situations full of risks – Purposefully doing your utmost – Every day a new challenge
2) PERSONAL-ORIENTED						JOB-ORIENTED
– Considering personal problems – Taking responsibility for the well-being of the employees – Decisions are taken by groups						– Putting a lot of pressure to finish the job – Performance is more important than the well-being of the employees – Decisions are taken by individuals
3) ORGANIZATIONALLY LINKED						PROFESIONAL
– Employees identify themselves with their organization – Employees do not look far ahead – Hiring people from the right family, social class, and educational background – Norms from work also count at home						– Employees identify with their profession – Employees look far ahead – Hiring people because of their ability for their work – Private life is everyone's own business
4) OPEN						CLOSED
– Openness against newcomers and outsiders – Nearly everyone fits in the organization – New employees feel quickly at home						– Closeness through mystery, even for their own employees – Only special people fit in the organization – New employees don't feel quickly at home
5) TIGHT CONTROL						EASY CONTROL
– Are aware of costs – Strictly sticking to meeting times – Seriously talking about work and the organization – There are strict codes for correct behavior						– Are not aware of costs – Approximately abiding by meeting times – Joking about the company and work – There are no firm conduct rules
6) PRAGMATIC						NORMATIVE
– Meeting the demands of the customers – Is guided by the market – Results are more important then procedures – Pragmatic ethical attitudes						– Correct use of procedures – Is guided by the appointed tasks – Procedures are more important then results – High ethical norms

9 An integral step by step plan for continuous improvement

This chapter describes an integral step by step plan for continuous control of the operational processes and successful implementation of the TQM-working method within the organization. This holistic plan comprises of the following 25 steps:

Step 1

Start with a three-day workshop, in which all managers get the opportunity to formulate their own personal mission, vision, and key roles of their lives. Expand this process to development of a common mission, vision, and core values of the whole organization. These common organizational mission, vision, and core values form the basis for developing the objectives, strategies, critical success factors, and performance indicators of the company (see figures 9.1 and 9.2). Next, balance your personal mission, vision, and key roles with the organizational mission, vision, and core values. In other words:

> **Personal (<mission>, <vision>, <key roles>) ≈ Organizational (<mission>, <vision>, <core values>)**

The following questions are important here: Are your personal mission, vision, and key roles represented in the organizational mission, vision, and core values? If not, should your personal mission, vision, and key roles be adjusted or expanded? Are they acceptable? How can they be developed in the organization? Are you prepared to look for another organization where these have a higher priority? The development of the personal and organizational mission, vision, and roles/values does not only take place at the management level, but at all lower organizational levels in a series of meetings. Everyone in the organization needs to be actively involved in this top-down and bottom-up process. This strategic management process will be discussed further in this chapter because adequate execution of this process is essential for successful implementation of TQM.

Personal mission, vision, and key roles

Each employee has to formulate his/her own personal mission, vision, and key roles. Formulate these elements in a positive and current manner, as if everything happens at this present moment. Your *personal mission statement* encompasses your life philosophy and says who you are, what your life goals are, why you live, and what your deepest aspirations are. Your *personal vision statement* is a description of where you're going, which values and principles guide you to reach

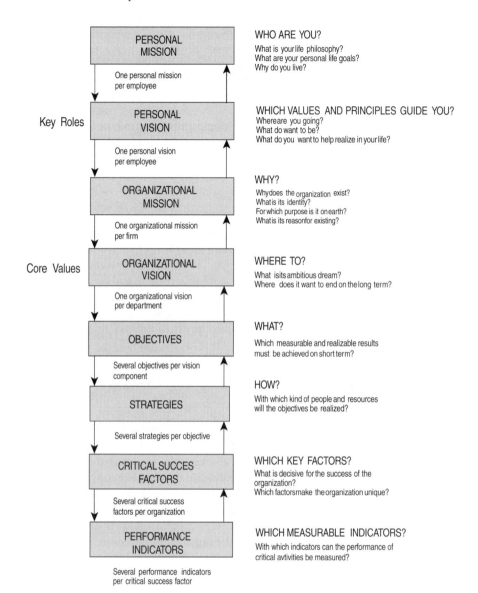

Figure 9.1 Personal and organizational mission and vision, as starting point in the strategic management process

that point, what you want to realize in your life, what ideal characteristics you would like to have, and what your ideal profession, living and health conditions are. Your key roles regard the way you fulfill or want to fulfill several roles in your life to realize your personal mission, such as the role of a father, mother, friend, manager, neighbor, etc. In other words, the relationships you would like to have with your friends, family, neighbors, and others. According to Stephen Covey

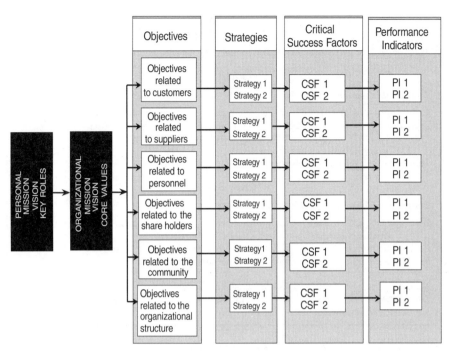

Figure 9.2 Stakeholders in the strategic management process

(1993), the whole of these three elements is sort of a constitution which guides your life, and forms the basis to evaluate decisions, what you want to be, and what you want to do. The way this is formulated motivates you to think deeply about your life, and gives meaning to everything you do. It helps you to discover your innermost feelings and clarifies what is important to you. You can eventually re-write these in case your living conditions or thinking patterns change in the course of several years. You can get an idea of your personal mission, vision, and key roles if you answer the following two questions: What would you like to have written on your tombstone? Which memories would you like to leave behind when you pass on? The following is an example of an effectively formulated personal mission, vision and key roles of a manager. This example is derived from the recommended book *"The seven habits of highly effective people"* by Stephen Covey (1993).

Personal Mission

My mission is to live with integrity and to make a difference in the lives of others.

Personal Vision

To fulfill this mission:

I have charity: I seek out and love the one –each one- regardless of his situation.
I sacrifice: I devote my time, talents, and resources to my mission.
I inspire: I teach by example that we are all children of a loving Heavenly Father and that
        every Goliath can be overcome.
I am impactful: What I do makes a difference in the lives of others.

Key Roles

These roles take priority in achieving my mission:

Husband: my partner is the most important person in my life. Together we contribute the
        fruits of harmony, industry, charity, and thrift.
Father: I help my children experience progressively greater joy in their lives.
Son/brother: I am frequently "there" for support and love.
Christian: God can count on me to keep my covenants and to serve his other children.
Neighbor: The love of Christ is visible through my actions toward others.
Change Agent: I am a catalyst for developing high performance in large organizations.
Scholar: I learn important new things every day.

Organizational mission, vision and core values

When formulating the common organizational mission, vision, and core values, the whole strategy development process needs to be taken into consideration. Introduction of TQM is one of the possible strategic options to strengthen your competitive position. The strategy development process comprises of a cycle of successive phases, which can be distinguished into *personal mission/vision development, organizational mission/vision development, situation analysis, strategy formulation, and planning & implementation* (Rampersad, 1997). Figure 9.3 shows a model representation of this cyclical process. The first step of this process has already been described. Next, the following phases will be discussed.

Organizational mission/vision development is the second phase in the strategy formation process, see figure 9.3. The central questions here are: why? and where to? *Organizational mission* encompasses the identity and the core competence of the firm and indicates its reasons for existence, for who it exists, why it exists, what its primary goal is, and who its most important stakeholders are (see figure 9.2). The mission is therefore not tied to time. An effective formulated mission creates unambiguous behavior of employees, strengthens one-mindedness, and improves the internal communication and the atmosphere within the organization. The accompanying illustrations show two effective organizational mission statements.

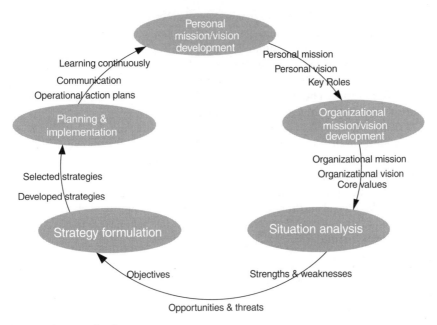

Figure 9.3 Strategy development process

Mission Hamilton-Wentworth Regional Police

Our mission is to serve and protect in partnership with our community.

Mission ESSO Imperial Oil

The company's mission is to create shareholder value through the development and sale of hydrocarbon energy and related products.

Organizational vision on the other hand encompasses a long-term dream of the firm and indicates the transformation path necessary to accomplish this (Senge, 1990). Vision is an image of the desired future. An effective formulated organizational vision gives direction to personal ambitions and creativity, creates a climate through drastic changes, strengthens belief in the future, and releases energy in people. The organizational vision is, contrary to the organizational mission, tied to a time horizon and the related concrete goals.

Effectively formulated organizational mission and vision statements meet the following criteria:

- Short, global, and abstract; it is understandable, communicable, and clear for everyone in the organization to serve as a concrete guideline for decisions.

- Organization specific; the emphasis is on distinctive elements with respect to other organizations. At the same time, the limits are widely formulated to allow development of new initiatives.
- Ambitious, challenging, motivating, and idealistic; inspires employees and gives direction to initiatives and creativity.
- Clarifies purpose and direction and gives meaning to the change expected of people; it aligns people toward a common goal.
- Realistic; it is recognizable to everyone. The feasibility is not open for discussion.
- Everybody in the organization is involved in the development process; this includes employees from the lowest to the highest.
- Mission is timeless and vision is linked to time.
- Aligned with company core values and linked to customer needs.
- It includes ethical starting points and cultural components, such as respect for the individual, make a contribution to society, help people to develop their opportunities, etc.

The organizational mission and vision together form an important management instrument that expresses the soul of the firm and indicates what the organization stands for, for which purpose it exists on earth, what its primary goal is, where it wants to go to, how it plans to reach there (based on its values), and on which important points should everyone concentrate. They form the collective ambition of the organization, and have an important impact on the bond of employees to the organization and their performance. A successfully formulated collective ambition shows people how their activities contribute to the whole, whereby they work together on the goal of the organization, which will lead to higher performances. As a result, they get a feeling of pride that they are making a useful contribution towards something that is worthwhile. This only works if they believe that management has a long-standing commitment to it. The organizational mission and vision give direction to a firm and functions as a compass and a road map. The convincing promotion of an active, inspiring, recognizable, challenging, and fascinating mission and vision that touches people and creates feelings of solidarity usually leads to more effort, satisfaction, and commitment. After all, such a common ambition inspires creativity, motivates and mobilizes people, gives them energy, and leads to improved performances. An organization will be successful if it succeeds in creating a sense, a meaning that releases energy in people, raises involvement and puts people in movement. Mission and vision as management instruments also offer the possibility of creating unity in the behavior of employees, to make employees feel proud of their organization, to let them focus on the relevant activities which create value for customers, and to eliminate non-productive activities. When a person does something which he finds meaningful then what he does will appeal to him. This generates more ability to be dynamic, creative, and task oriented. An effective organizational mission and vision also establishes a foundation for decision making and helps managers with decisions concerning the use of available resources. In an organization without a mission and vision, people are exposed to ad-hoc decisions and short-term changes. That's why it is important that each individual demonstrates belief in the organization's mission and ownership of its vision. The concepts of organizational mission and vision are further worked out in table 9.1.

Table 9.1 Organizational mission/vision concept

Common ambition	Core	Aspects	Meaning to employees
Mission	**WHY?** – Identity and core competence of the organization – Its reasons for existence – Its ultimate primary goal – For who does it exist – Why it's on earth – Its most important stakeholders	– Primary goal – Stakeholders – Reasons for existence Not tied to a time horizon.	– For what purpose do I work there? – Can I identify myself with the working methods, which are used? – Why do we find it meaningful or valuable that our organization exists? – What do the employees want to mean for each other and the surroundings? – Which added value do they want to deliver? Thus: giving a meaning, identification, and similarly oriented
Vision	**WHERE TO?** – Display of a common notion of a desired and a feasibly considered future situation – Formulation of the long term ambition (strategic intent) – Notion of the transformation path that is needed to reach that dream – the core values that underlie the actions of the organization	– New developments – Ambitions – Future path – Core values – Direction – Destination Tied to a time horizon. Tied to concrete and measurable goals.	– Where are we going together? – What is the desired long-term perspective of the organization? – Is linked to the personal ambitions of employees Thus: giving direction to personal ambitions and creativity, creating an environment for drastic changes, strengthening believe in the future (and with that release energy), strengthening one mindedness and unity of behavior.

The organizational vision is also linked to a number of core values, in order to strengthen the one-mindedness of the employees, and favorably influence their behavior and the organizational culture. *By sharing these values, a group becomes a team and a company becomes a community.* The core values determine what approach is used to realize the vision. They determine how we treat each other, and how we see our clients, employees, the community, and our suppliers. After all, values in an organization usually inspire commitment, loyalty, and devotion in all parts of the organization. It is also recognized that the efforts and involvement of people are usually optimal if their own principles and that of the organization match each other. A number of possible core values are shown in table 9.2 (Rampersad, 1998).

Table 9.2 Core values

Core values
Our organization will be guided by the following core values, which are embedded in its standards:
Integrity: we will be honest with our customers, suppliers, employees, shareholders and the community of which we are part. What is said will also be done, an agreement is an agreement.
Customer satisfaction: we will continuously listen to our customers and provide them with products/services of a quality that they expect of us, and we will continuously delight them.
Commitment: we will work with dedicated people and completely stand behind everything we do.
Respect: we will appreciate each other, acknowledge each other, treat each other as equal, and respect each other.
Professionalism: we will continuously strive for superior performances in everything our organization undertakes.
Teamwork: we will work harmoniously together, help each other, be mutually responsible, and support each other.
Trust: nothing is a secret.
Skilled: we will continuously improve the capacities and creativity of our employees.
Entrepreneurial: we will be innovative, creative and flexible, take well calculated risks, take initiative, learn from our mistakes, and continuously improve ourselves.
Empowerment: we will be resolute and understand what responsibility and effort means, as well as sympathize with the needs of our employees.

To illustrate the use of core values in real life, an example is given here from the Life Administration Group (part of the Home Service Division of the Prudential Assurance Co. Ltd. in the UK), whereby the organization mission was translated to a set of easy-to-understand core values (Oakland, 1995). The formulation of these values forms their way of life statements.

Organizational mission and core values of Life Administration Group (Prudential Assurance Co. Ltd.)

Mission

We administer Prudential Assurance life business. Our purpose is to delight our customers by delivering a quality service, in a cost-effective manner, through the contribution of everyone.

Core values

We are committed to delivering a quality service to our customers:

- The customer is the reason we exist and the key consideration in carrying out our day-to-day business.
- The customer is the person or area to whom we are providing a service.
- Everyone is a vital link in the service chain and the successful partnership between the suppliers of services and their customers is of primary importance.
- As individuals and teams we demonstrate our commitment to our customers by "getting it right first time".
- We will continually review, redefine and improve the quality of service we provide to meet the changing expectations of our customers.

We recognize that our purpose can only be achieved trough people:

- We recognize that everyone wants to provide a quality service.
- Each individual has the right to know what is expected of him/her and the reasons why.
- We are committed to providing continuous education, training and development opportunities to enable everyone to realize their full potential.
- Each individual is responsible for providing a quality service.
- We encourage people throughout the organization to listen actively to each other and to voice their ideas and opinions.

We are committed to creating a business-like and caring working environment:

- We will communicate in an open manner, which mirrors and supports our way of life.
- Teamwork will play a vital part in achieving our purpose.
- Opportunity will be given to individuals and teams to make changes at the level where it is most practical.
- We actively support the local community and the wider environment in which we live and work.

The organizational mission, vision and guiding principles of Coca-Cola's Central America & Caribbean Division are described in the next frame, to illustrate the above.

Organizational mission, vision and guiding principles of Coca-Cola's Central America & Carribean Division

Mission

We exist to create value for our share owners on a sustainable basis be meeting specific business objectives which enhance the value of our brands. We have an obligation to lead our partners in this system to marketing efforts which focus on the consumer, are executed in a timely fashion and leverage the individual and combined strengths of all system partners.

Vision 1: Work environment

Things have really changed around here. We have a special culture in this division where integrity and honesty are more than guiding principles – they are a way of life. Trust and mutual respect abound, so we are all comfortable taking risks. We have a credible reward system, with clear accountability for, and recognition of, results. Clarity pervades our working lives. We know where we are going, and focus on getting there. People have a sense of purpose, and share ideas with each other about how to get results. We understand our roles, and accept responsibility for our actions. We get lots of support from other departments, and are not afraid to ask for help. We have not had a real crisis in a while, and there is enough time to get our work done. We are always learning and developing. We get exposure to all aspects of the business, and can see how our careers can grow. Many of our collagues have moved on to bigger jobs elsewhere. It boils down to teamwork. We are all important, understand each other, and are sprinting down parallel paths to the same destination. Our bottlers and suppliers are starting to act just like us. I guess that is what high performance is all about. It sure is fun!

Vision2: Consumer

Coca-Cola soft drinks are an important part of my life. They are the best tasting, highest quality drinks, and I can always find them, cold, when I am thirsty. They refresh my mind, body, and spirit. We have a unique bond, and Coca Cola soft drinks are always there to share my special moments with. I feel that Coca Cola listens to me, respects me, and understands me. I prefer Coca Cola soft drinks, and this is reinforced every time I drink one. My family accepts no substitutes. Coca Cola is number one.

Vision3: Customer

Coca-Cola is the best supplier I have. They are always adding value to my business. They have the best brands, the best marketing, and never fail to provide the best service. They have generated tons of traffic for my stores, and my soft drink profits have doubled in the past three years. I feel I have a unique relationship with Coca-Cola. They are fair and honest, and they really care about me. I trust them, and I am proud to sell Coca-Cola products. Come to think of it. Coca-Cola is more than my best supplier. They are really my partners.

Vision 4: Competitor

Coca-Cola is unbeatable. They have redefined the game, and they lead it. They are innovative, aggressive, fast focused, and great at execution. They are well organized, and staffed to create value with great marketing. Coca-Cola is a first class act. They operate with integrity. I can not compete with them head on. I do not make any money, and I am close to bankruptcy. It is really frustrating. I am always following them, scrambling to survive.

Vision 5: Community

Coca-Cola is a good neighbor. They are socially responsible, environmentally sensitive, and concerned about improving the quality of our lives. They are a big taxpayer here, and have created lots of jobs in our community. This has had a multiplier effect on our local economy. Coca-Cola is a model employer. I hope my kids can work there someday.

Vision 6: Results

Our business results have been constantly above budget and above average for the company. We are capturing all the growth, and have been growing unit cases at 15% per year. Operating income and economic profit have both doubled in the past three years. We have leadership in all our markets. And are on track to double our per capita by 2005

Guiding principles

We achieve a shared vision and alignment with our existing bottler partners.

We recruit, develop and retain for the global system the most qualified human capital necessary to meet our presen and futurre business needs. Our employees reflect racial, cultural and gender make-up of our consumers.

We recognize that all communication (internal and external) needs to be clear and precise, especially in an environment of multiple languages.

We create a culture of which rewards innovation, new ideas, and intelligent risk taking (with cleraly defined accountability).

We treat all our associates, bottlers, customers and external constituents with respect, honesty, candor, and integrity.

In practice, top management and middle management develop the conceptual overall organization mission, vision, objectives, and strategies. This draft strategic policy is than communicated to the other employees through different workshops on all levels. Brainstorming takes place in teams, whereby each team reflects on the entire organization. After an eventual adjustment of the draft, it gets a formal status. This way the employees get a better insight into the course to be followed by the organization. After having completed this process, each department or unit formulates their own specific vision, objectives, and strategies, which are attuned

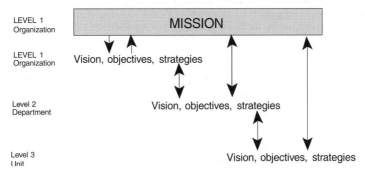

Figure 9.4 Organizational mission translated to lower organizational levels

to the common organizational mission (see figure 9.4). The basic idea here is that each organizational level should have the same mission. This way, the message from top management is communicated downwards in a consistent manner. This top-down and bottom-up strategy forming process occurs repeatedly on all subsequent organizational levels in increasing detail. The strategies formulated by employees at a higher level are considered as vision and objectives by personnel at a lower level. Thus the HOW from one is the WHERE and WHAT of another, or the strategies of the higher layer of management become the vision and objectives of the next level down. This also implies that the vision and goals formulated by a lower level can be seen as a means to realize strategies by a higher level. In this manner, the overall strategic business plan is systemically translated into more specific plans at each organizational level.

Situation analysis is the next step in the strategy forming process and concerns the evaluation of the strategic position of the organization and documentation of the organization's objectives (see figure 9.3). In this phase, the strengths and weaknesses of the organization (internal) and the opportunities and threats from the environment (external) are first brought into perspective. This is called a SWOT-analysis, which stands for *Strengths, Weaknesses, Opportunities, and Threats*. Benchmarking is an important instrument here that is focused on improving performances with respect to the leading competitor. Next, the objectives (intended short-term results) are determined, whereby the *what* is central (see figure 9.1). In this process, all stakeholders (such as customers, suppliers, employees, shareholders, etc.), should be taken into consideration (see figure 9.2). The most important objectives with regard to the different stakeholders are shown in the following frame.

- *Customers:* increasing leadership with respect to quality and service level. A competitive price/performance ratio.
- *Personnel:* a working climate, which is inspiring, challenging, and enjoyable. Focused on increasing labor productivity, improving motivation, decreasing absenteeism due to illness, and protecting the employee's wellbeing. Thus, an improved quality of labor.
- *Organizational structure:* decreasing costs and shortening throughput time based on improved efficiency.
- *Suppliers:* effective partnership relation with suppliers in order to improve the quality, decrease the purchase costs, increase the added value, and shorten the delivery time.
- *Society:* educational system, employment, eco-conscious, and energy consumption.
- *Shareholders:* increasing the positive cash flow (= sales - {costs + tax}), decreasing the cost of capital provision, a superior return on all investments and thus, an improved shareholder's value.

The objectives are derived directly from the organizational vision and form realizable milestones, which are measured yearly. Each vision part has one or more goals. These are formulated at top management level as well as on department level, in order to realize the vision. Organizational objectives are usually based on a business economics approach, such as sales growth, market share, profitability, productivity, quality, etc. Because the intended result is reflected by a goal, the formulation of this must be *SMART; Specific, Measurable, Achievable, Realistic,* and *Time specific*. Examples of SMART-goals are: *an increase of 6% in the market share of product B in South America within two years, achieve a market growth of 6-7 % for the next 2 years, reduce the waste-percentage from 3% to 0.5% within one year, improve delivery reliability by 50% within six months, reduce the service call rate by 25% per year for the next three years, reduce the throughput time from 8,5 days to 1 day in ten months.*

Strategy formulation is the next phase in the strategy development process (see figure 9.3), whereby alternative strategies are developed and choices are made, based on the visible gap between the present and desired situation. The who is central here (see figure 9.1). Strategy indicates how the objectives can be realized and which choices should be made. It is the answer of the SWOT-analysis. Do here only what you're unique in and outsource the supporting activities to specialists, who can do it better, quicker, and cheaper than you can. Other examples of creative strategies are: *increasing shareholder value through e-business, focusing on customer relationships, value chain integration, and restructuring the compensation, recognition, and reward policies* (Deise, et al., 2000). Strategies are linked to the objectives per stakeholder, as is seen in figure 9.2. These strategies should then be translated into *Critical Success Factors (CSFs)*. These *key factors* are essential to the continuation of the organization and thus, require constant attention from management. They determine the competitive advantage of the organization because they are strongly related to its core competencies. Examples of CSFs are: *high product quality, good customer service, motivated & skilled people, and short time-to-market*. Results of benchmark-studies and inventories of customer's data form the most important inputs for determining CSFs. After the CSFs are determined, Performance Indicators (PIs) are derived from them. These *measurable quantities* measure the performances of critical activities. The CSFs and PIs will be further discussed, in phases 4, 7, and 8 of this step by step plan.

Planning and implementation is the last phase in the cycle (see figure 9.3) and concerns the introduction of chosen strategies, which result in a strategic business plan, operational department plans, and concrete projects. In this last phase of the strategy development process, the chosen strategies are translated into operational plans for the different departments or units within the organization, after which they will be implemented (see figure 9.4). The actions to be undertaken are worked out in the operational plans for the different business functions for a period of one year. It is a short-term plan and tactically of nature. The central question is: what must financing, HRM, purchasing, marketing, R&D, logistics, production, maintenance, and services do to realize the overall organizational mission, vision, objectives, and strategies? The business objectives are worked out by the different departments according to investments, production costs, new technologies, production capacities, production volume, stock, supplier selection, outsourcing, required education, etc. The use of project management techniques is usually necessary during this phase, as well as creating awareness for change.

The organizational mission, vision, objectives, and strategies of Oil Refinery Shell Pernis (Rotterdam) are described in the adjoining frame, to illustrate the above.

Organizational mission, vision, objectives, and strategies of Shell Oil Refinery Pernis

In 1998, Shell Pernis has taken it upon itself to be a world class refinery: a refinery with a perfect operation that belongs to the best in Europe and the top in the Benelux. To achieve this, plan PERFECT '98 was launched in mid 1996 within the organization to change and attune the organization optimally to the dynamics of the market. Here, the decentralization of the functional structure was central, whereby the activities were organized as much as possible around the primary process, which is "the production of oil and chemical products for Shell companies". The starting points of this organizational change are given below.

MISSION
Profitable production of oil and chemical products for Shell companies all over the world.

VISION
To achieve the mission Shell Pernis wants to be a large producer who:
1. Is efficient, cheap, and as such competitive.
2. Works customer oriented and delivers the agreed upon quality.
3. Acts safe and eco-conscious.
4. Offers employees challenging work in a decisive organization.

From the tought that employees eventually determine the success of the company, it is of the greatest interest that the organization of Shell Pernis is set up in such a way that the talents of all employees are taken advantage off. To belong to the best in the industry, everything within the company will be focused on achieving high productivity with a motivated working community.

OBJECTIVES
Shell Pernis as pacesetter in the mentioned fields, will have to comply with a number of goals. These goals are derived from the four vision elements and are directed at the hardware as well as the software:

1. Regarding 'efficient, cheap, and as such competitive':
   • fixed costs within budget and decreasing yearly in real terms;
   • per factory, not more than three days unplanned shut downs;
   • working with a team that is under the manpower norm;
   • improving corrected energy & loss index with 1 point per year;
   • maintenance costs on average 25% lower than in 1995.

2. Regarding 'customer oriented and delivers the agreed upon quality':
   • decreasing the number of customers complaints/claims with 25% per year;
   • all departments certified by 1997;
   • percentage followed through advises above 90%;
   • 95% of the assignments delivered within "service levels".

3. Regarding 'safe and eco-conscious':
   • a yearly total recordable case frequency and lost time injury frequency that is 10% lower than the best results of the previous years;
   • absenteeism due to illness of less than 2%;
   • a continuous reduction of the number of complaints from neighbors;
   • decreasing the number of environmental incidents per year with at least 25%;
   • no litter outside the wastebaskets.

4. Regarding 'challenging work in a decisive organization':
   • at least 80% of all employees find that they have challenging work;
   • at least 80% of all employees find that they work under good management.

STRATEGIES
The vision will be realized through the following approach:

1. Regarding 'efficient, cheap, and as such competitive':
   • focus on the financial company results in the short and long run;
   • using energy and raw materials efficiently;

- securing integrity of the installation;
- attuning maintenance optimally to the desired user-goals;
- benchmarking with the best in the industry.

2. Regarding *'customer oriented and delivers the agreed upon quality'*:
   - attuning delivery of products and services with internal and external customers, contractors and suppliers;
   - certifying the core activities according to IOS-norms.

3. Regarding *'safe and eco-conscious'*:
   - maintaining a clean and cheerful plant;
   - protecting the health and wellbeing of employees;
   - realizing that accidents and incidents can be prevented (working unsafe = shut down);
   - preventing negative influences on the environment as much as possible.

4. Regarding *'challenging work in an decisive organization'*:
   - effective communication of the company's goals to all employees;
   - result oriented actions based on personal goals and company goals;
   - developing employees purposiveness;
   - economically optimize the division between outsourcing and in-house production;
   - offering stable employment for those who distinguish themselves in performance and added value;
   - yearly communication of the agreements with shareholders and of actual results;
   - introduction of a 180° personnel assessment system;
   - delegated responsibilities and authorties as far as possible within the organization.

Step 2

Develop a quality policy based on the results of step one. Management must communicate these results and the quality policy directly and clearly to all employees at all levels of the organization in a series of meetings. They must make sure that the company values are the driving force for the attitude and behavior of everyone. Management must announce the start of TQM, as part of the quality policy, and prove that they are committed to it. An example of an effective quality policy is given below (Oakland, 1995).

Quality policy

- Quality improvement is primarily the responsibility of management.
- In order to involve everyone in the organization in quality improvement, management will enable all employees to participate in the preparation, implementation and evaluation of improvement activities.
- Quality improvement will be tackled and followed up in a systematic and planned manner. This applies to every part of our organization.
- Quality improvement will be a continuous process.
- The organization will concentrate on its customers and suppliers, both external and internal.
- The performance of our competitors will be shown to all relevant units.
- Important suppliers will be closely involved in our quality policy. This relates to both external and internal suppliers of goods, resources, and services.
- Widespread attention will be given to education and training activities, which will be assessed with regard to their contribution to the quality policy.
- Publicity will be given to the quality policy in every part of the organization so that everyone may understand it. All available methods and media will be used for its internal and external promotion and communication.
- Reporting on the progress of the implementation of the policy will be a permanent agenda item in management meetings.

Step 3

Create a TQM-infrastructure and develop a TQM-mentality and awareness throughout the entire organization. Install a TQM-steering group, introduce the *sponsorship* concept and appoint a TQM-manager. Next, train all employees in TQM, in multidisciplinary groups of 10 to 15 participants, with this book as a reference guide. Start with top management and middle management (TQM-steering group). An external TQM consultant, in collaboration with the appointed TQM-manager can eventually facilitate this first training. The director, in collaboration with the TQM-manager must facilitate the second session. Then, the TQM-manager appoints a participant from the first group each time to train the next group. The groups should have a well-balanced make-up of employees from different departments and all levels of the organization. These internal workshops are given every two or three weeks during normal working hours for three to four working days. The following step can start right after the first group (steering group) has been trained. The routinely use of TQM can be stimulated by introducing a TQM-pocket book, in which the most important methods and techniques are included. This can also be used during the workshops. Every person in the organization must become aware of the need to improve, what TQM is, and why it is important to you and your organization. Inform your customers and suppliers also, and explain why you are making changes, and how your activities will affect them.

Step 4

Translate the organizational mission, vision, goals, and strategies into critical success factors (see figures 9.2 and 9.3); a Critical Success Factor is one in which the organization must be outstanding to be able to survive, or that which is of decisive importance to the success of the organization. These factors determine the competitive advantage of an organization. They are factors that make the organization unique on the market. Based on this, the organization can be guided effectively. Examples of CSFs are: *highly motivated and skilled employees, customer orientation, high product quality, good control of costs, rapidity of bringing a new product on the market (time-to-market), efficient dealers' organization, good customer service, complete product assortment, eco-consciousness, and availability of certain facilities.* Such factors can be critical to the success or failure of an organization. They should be determined through brainstorming with the entire management team, and they should be hierarchically arranged. The operational processes which are eligible for quality improvement, are to an important degree dependent on the CSFs of the organization.

Step 5

Determine the operational processes through brainstorming in several workshops. An operational process is characterized by:

- An input. For example information, energy, personnel, skills, knowledge, capital, material, resources, services, etc.

Business processes form a series of activities, which are executed by different business functions. These processes are focused on delivering a product or service to an internal or external customer.

Examples of business processes in a production company are:
- Developing products; identifying of and communicating with customers, determine the customer's needs, product design, process design, attuning service processes to it, etc.
- Purchasing from suppliers; selection of suppliers, closing a purchasing contract, receiving purchasing invoices, receiving goods, etc.
- Selling to customers ; making sales planning, acquisition, making offers, processing the order, invoicing the order, etc.

Figure 9.5 Business processes

- A defined process. Regards a series of linked actions, transforming input from suppliers into output for customers. A process is the transformation of a set of inputs into outputs that satisfy customer needs and expectations. All activities, physical and intellectual, can be viewed as processes.
- An output. Products, services, information, and paperwork.
- The possession of internal/external customers and suppliers. A process without customers is unnecessary.

An organization can be considered to be a chain of related activities. Each organizational process forms a series of activities which are fulfilled by different operational functions (see figure 9.5), such as for example *making rooms available (in a hotel), developing products (in a production company), purchasing from a supplier (in a trading company), processing data (in a bank)*, etc. Make a distinction between key processes (primary processes) and non-key processes (supporting processes). Key processes start and end with the customer and are focused on adding value for the customer, such as the above mentioned processes. Non-key factors are supportive of nature, such as the activities of the financial affairs, and the maintenance department.

Step 6

Per operational process, make a detailed division in sub-processes and process sections up to the level of action. Start with key processes. For example, the production process in an industrial company can be divided into the sub-processes *of fabricating, assembling, spraying paint, testing, and packaging. The sub-process fabricating can then be sub-divided in the process sections supplying, sorting, sawing, drilling, bending, sanding*, etc. Supplying can again be divided in the activities *picking up, moving, putting down, fastening*, etc.

Step 7

Determine with the aid of a matrix, which operational processes are relevant from the standpoint of the CSFs. If a process is essential, this is marked in the matrix, see also (Nijhuis van, et al., 1996). Table 9.3 shows an example of this exercise. By using this, an illustration is obtained of the most important processes that add value for the customer. Processes that create a high added value receive most attention and are eligible for continuous improvement. Non-essential processes (those with hardly any marks in the matrix) can better be outsourced.

Table 9.3 Matrix CSFs and operational processes

Operational processes	Critical success factors (CSFs)			
	Motivated employees	Customer orientation	Product quality	Cost control
1. Purchasing				
1.1 selecting suppliers	x	x	x	x
1.2 closing purchasing contract	x		x	x
1.3 placing purchasing order				x
1.4 receiving goods and purchasing invoices				x
1.5 paying purchasing invoices				x
2. Fabricating				
2.1 supplying	x	x	x	
2.2 sorting	x	x	x	
2.3 sawing	x	x	x	x
2.4 drilling	x	x	x	
2.5 bending	x	x	x	
2.6 sanding	x	x	x	
3. Assembling	x	x	x	x
4. Spraying paint	x	x	x	x
5. Testing	x	x	x	
6. Packaging	x	x	x	x
7. Selling				
7.1 acquisition	x	x		x
7.2 order processing				
7.3 distributing			x	
8. Administration	x			

Step 8

Determine per process-CSF-combination one or more Performance Indicators (PIs). A Performance Indicator is a measurable quantity of an activity, which is related to a certain CSF and on which basis the performance of the organization can be evaluated. PI measures the activities that are of crucial importance to the organization and consequently, deliver a valuable contribution to controlling the operational processes (see also table 6.4). They give management timely signals regarding the efficient operation of the organization based on measurements of process changes and comparisons between the measurement results and the norms. PIs are linked to the organizational goals through the CSFs and the strategies (see figures 9.2 and 9.3). The following PIs belong to a customer oriented organization: *number of customer's complaints, the speed with which complaints are dealt with, repair time, % complete deliveries that are on time and according to the specifications,* and *the related throughput time of orders.* The PIs that are linked to a high product quality (CSF) are for example: *number of customer complaints, % rejects, % returns of damaged goods, number of process interruptions,* and *the availability of machines.* The following PIs pertain to motivated employees: *% absence due to illness, % late comers, added value per personnel costs,* and *labor productivity.* Table 9.4 shows an example whereby per process-CSF-combination, one or more possible PIs are given.

Table 9.4 Organizational process/CSFs and performance indicators (PIs) matrix

Operational processes	Critical Success Factors (CSFs)			
	Motivated employees	Customer orientation	Product quality	Cost control
1. Purchasing	– % personell turnover – labor productivity	– invoicing speed – throughput time	– % approved materials	– purchase share as % of sales – purchase price vs. market price
2. Fabricating	– % absence due to illness – labor productivity – added value per personnel costs – training costs as % of sales	– number of customer complaints – throughput time – delivery reliability	– % rejects – % waste – effectiveness – ISO norms – added value – % damaged – quality grade	– availability of machines – % failures – efficiency – quality costs – capital productivity – material productivity – added value per labor time – operational costs as % of sales

Table 9.4 (Continued)

3. Selling				
3.1 acquisition	– % sales per sales person – labor productivity	– number of customer complaints – market shares – market growth	– number of customer complaints – % sales from new products	– efficiency – productivity
3.2 order processing	– order throughput time – labor productivity	– turnover speed – invoicing speed – % of delayed orders	– delivery reliability	– efficiency – productivity – added value per labor time
3.3 distributing	– % absence due to illnesses – labor productivity – % personell turnover	– % complete deliveries, on time, and according to specifications – delivery speed	– % returns of damaged goods – effectiveness	– circulation velocity of stocks – warehouse utilization – stock levels – availability of transportation systems – capital productivity
4. Administrating	– labor productivity	– response time to a service request – number of customer complaints	– effectiveness	– billing speed – debtors age – efficiency

Step 9

Quantify the PIs by completing analyses and measurements and by using these, make an estimate of the performance of the processes; indicate which process scores high or low. Identify the expectations of the customer through a customer inquiry; also make an inventory of the customer complaints through surveys, and submit these complaints to an organizational process; complaints regarding timely and complete delivery, communication, meeting the demands, etc. Define the problem clearly and understandably.

Step 10

Let the TQM-steering group select the critical processes that cause most of the complaints from external customers, as well as processes that have a low PI-score and create high added value for customers. Identify the most promising opportunities for improvement. Start with the project that has the highest chance of success, because the first quality improvement projects have to set an example. Start the process at the highest possible level and cascade it through the organization, layer by layer, to ensure thorough adoption of this improvement philosophy.

Step 11

Install a quality improvement team per selected process, consisting of a team leader, a TQM-facilitator, and other team members. Let the sponsor (in the steering group) select the other team members together with the team leader. The team must start off with a clear statement of the objective they hope to achieve. Train the team continuously in the use of quality improvement techniques and methods, as well as in the fields of teamwork and project management. Give the team the ownership over their process, and let them describe the relevant process and identify it in details. Determine the existing execution of tasks and make a division in sub- and partial processes. Flow chart these processes and identify the customer/supplier relationships. Create time for the team and give all individuals the resources they need to fulfil their responsibility for the quality of their processes.

Step 12

Evaluate the current working method and make an inventory of the degree of process control, based on the performance indicators. Central questions here are: what kind of work is completed now, why, where, when, by whom, and how? Can certain activities be eliminated, simplified, combined, altered, reorganized, executed parallel, or outsourced? Is the infrastructure in a good state, are the labor conditions good, is the layout efficient, and are the processes clearly defined? List the shortcomings (bottlenecks) of internal customers, that lead to unsatisfied external customers and increased quality costs.

Step 13

Evaluate the listed shortcomings with the aid of the performance indicators.

Step 14

List per selected shortcoming the causes and effects (per sub-process). Make for instance use of FMEA (determining cause-effect) and the fishbone diagram (to arrange causes).

Step 15

Select the causes to be eliminated based on success and priorities or importance. Also make use of the Pareto-analysis.

Step 16

Document the present known and best working method in standard procedures.

Step 17

Generate alternative solutions for the causes of shortcomings. Determine per solution (improvement):

a) the quality costs caused by the shortcoming;
b) the chances of success; estimate based on a number between 0 and 10 (see table 3.6);
c) the costs linked to the solution;
d) the time needed for implementation of the solution.

Cross the solution that is not cost-effective and calculate the Priority index

$$P = \frac{a \times b}{c \times d}$$

for the other solutions. Solutions with the highest Priority index have priority in being implemented. The organizational culture should also be considered. While selecting solutions, also make a costs and benefit analysis and determine the consequences of implementation in advance. Examine also the intangible benefits, such as a better working environment and more-satisfied people.

Steps 1 till 17 are related to the PLAN-phase

Step 18

First, implement the chosen solution on a limited scale and test it.

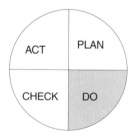

Step 18 is related to the DO-phase

Step 19

Check if the improvement was successfull. Evaluate the results from the solution with the help of performance indicators, and check to which degree the goals have been realized. Start again if necessary.

Step 19 is related to the CHECK-phase

Step 20

Introduce the proven improvement; implement the solution and improve the process.

Step 21

Review the results and document the improved process execution in standard procedures or working instructions. This involves documenting the successful solution in a new process standard and communicating it to everyone involved in the process. Train employees in the use of these procedures, so they know how to act according to these instructions. Urge employees to work according to the documented procedures.

Step 22

Measure and evaluate the process to be sure that it is controlled. Evaluate data and customer complaints and hold internal audits as well. Continuously monitor the improved process.

Step 23

Verify that there is in fact an implemented TQM-working method and a controlled process. If this is satisfactory, then follows a final presentation of the team results for the TQM-steering group, followed by certification of the process by the TQM-steering group. Evaluation of teamwork and rewarding of the obtained results are also part of this step. Identify and document any lessons you have learned about the improvement process itself.

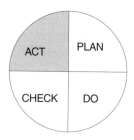

Step 20 till 23 are related to the ACT-phase

Step 24

Go back to step 10 for the installation of the next improvement team for the description and improvement of the next critical process. Naturally, you don't have to wait until the previous two steps have been completed. The implementation of TQM can run parallel at more than one location within the organization. Strive to make each individual in the organization a part of at least one improvement team.

Go frequently back to step 1 to up-date the formulated organization goals and strategies, based on the constantly changing environment.

Step 25

Eventually introduce a Process Improvement Team (PIT) to continuously improve and maintain the processes made controllable by the improvement team.

10 Concluding comments

This book is intended to be both a foundation and roadmap towards the implementation and maintenance of Total Quality Management in any organization. The learning objectives outlined in the introduction should have been met to your satisfaction. Consequently, after reading this book, you should now be able to:

Learning Objectives
➤ Better adapt your working method to the realization of total quality.
➤ Be acquainted with the tools and techniques within the context of your problem solving discipline and with their application within your organization.
➤ Develop interpersonal skills and apply these in all areas of your work.
➤ Successfully generate innovative ideas
➤ Effectively work as a team and coach teams successfully.
➤ Become an effective leader.
➤ Create a work climate in which people are happy, productive, and continuously learning from mistakes.
➤ Execute quality improvement process in a multidisciplinary and structured manner in order to solve organizational problems in a holistic way.
➤ Continuously control the quality of your products and services.
➤ Reduce your production costs.
➤ Improve your customer orientation.
➤ Deal with quality projects based on an inspiring personal and organizational mission, vision, related core values, and SMART goals.
➤ Deal with resistance against organizational changes and how to introduce a cultural change in your organization.
➤ Successfully coordinate the implementation of TQM.
➤ Maximize the opportunities of e-business and e-commerce.
➤ Continuously increase shareholder value.

This book should not be one that an executive or employee reads and then files in his/her library or hands over to a friend or colleague, never to be returned. It is expected that this book should become a reference manual to be used by organizations (big and small, private and public) as a guide to continuously improving the operation of their organization. Many of the tools and techniques outlined in this book are utilized daily on an "ad hoc" within successful organizations.

However, this book formalizes these tools and techniques and makes them available for utilization and implementation. All employees within the organization should become aware of these tools and techniques as methods to improve operations, produce better products and services, increase customer and employee satisfaction and generally improve both the overall social and economic environment within the organization.

Businesses must be aware that they have to not only keep up-to-date with customer needs and industry "best practices", but also to anticipate changes in these areas. Organizations that do not look to the future and/or do not routinely introduce necessary changes in anticipation of, or changes to, their operational environment are destined to fail. The most successful organizations are those that deal with change on a routine basis and utilize TQM or a similar process to ensure that their products and/or services continue to meet or exceed the expectations of their customers. Let's hope that your organization is one of these.

Bibliography

Barton, G.M., *Communication: Manage words effectively,* Personnel Journal 69, Costa Mesa, 1990.

Boyett, J.H. & J.T. Boyett, *The Guru Guide; the best ideas of the top management thinkers,* John Wiley & Sons, New York, 1998.

Camp, R.C., *Benchmarking: Searching for the best working methods that will lead to superior performances,* Kluwer Business information, Deventer, 1992.

Covey, S.R., *The seven habits of highly effective people,* Simon & Schuster, New York, 1993.

Craig, C. & C.Harris, *Productivity concepts and measurements; a managerial viewpoint,* Massachusetts Institute of Technology, Cambridge, Massachusetts, 1972.

Crosby, Ph.B., *Quality is Free,* McGraw-Hill, New York, 1984.

Culligan, M.J. et. al., *Back to Basics Management: The lost Craft of Leadership,* Facts on File Inc. New York, 1983.

Deise, M.V. et al., *Executive Guide to E-business; from tactics to strategy,* John Wiley & Sons, New York, 2000

Deming, W.E., *Out of the crisis,* Massachusetts Institute of Technology, Cambridge, Massachusetts, 1985.

Does, R.J.M. et al., *Statistical process control in business,* Kluwer Business information, Deventer, 1996.

Drucker, P., *Innovation and entrepreneurship. practice and principles,* Harper & Row, New York, 1985.

Drucker, P., *Post-capitalist Society,* Butterworth/Heinemann, Oxford, 1993.

Galpin, T., *Connecting Culture to Organizational Change,* HRMagazine, March 1996, pp. 84-90.

Gardner, J., *On Leadership,* Free Press, New York, 1990, pp. 48-53.

Geier, J.G. & D.E. Downey, *Energetics of Personality,* Aristos Publishing House, Minesota, 1989.

Gilbert, T.F., *Human competence: Engineering worthy performance,* McGraw-Hill, 1987.

Grootte, G.P. et. al., *Managing projects,* Spectrum/Marka, Utrecht, 1996.

Hamel, G. & C.K. Prahalad, *Competing for the Future; Breakthrough strategies for seizing control of your industry and creating markets of tomorrow,* Harvard Business School Press, Boston, 1994.

Harrison, R., *Understanding your organization character,* Harvard Business Review, May-June, Boston, 1972.

Hauser, J.R. & D.Clausing, *The house of quality,* Harvard Business Review, vol. 66,3, Boston, 1988.

Hoevenaars, A.M. et al., *Towards simplicity in organizations; working with self guiding units,* Kluwer Business information, Deventer, 1995.

Hofstede, G., *All thinks differently; handling culture differences,* Contact, Amsterdam, 1991.

Honey, P. & A. Mumford, *Manual of Learning Styles,* Honey, Maidenhead, 1992.

Imai, M., Kaizen, *Random House,* New York, 1986.

Ishikawa, K., *What is Total Quality Control? The Japanese way*, Prentice-Hall, Englewood Cliffs, 1985.

Jacobs, R.F., *Real Time Strategic Change,* Berrett-Koehler, San Francisco, 1994.

Kotter, J.P., *Leading Change,* Harvard Business School Press, Boston, 1996.

Loo, van der, J., *Dynamics in working relations: the four elements of cooperation and management,* De Toorts, Haarlem, 1995.

Maslow, A.H., *Motivation and Personality,* Harper & Row, New York, 1970.

NEN-ISO 9000-4, *Guidelines for quality improvement,* 1993.

Nijhuis van, C. et al., *Internal announcements; mirror of the organization, in the series "Controlling in practice".* Kluwer Business information, Deventer, 1996.

Oakland, J.S., *Total Quality Management,* Butterworth Heineman, Oxford, 1995.

O'Tool, J., *Leading Change: The argument for values-based leadership,* Ballantine Books, New York, 1996.

PA Consulting Group, *TQM-manual,* London, 1991.

Pareek, U & T.V. Rao, *Performance coaching,* in: T.W. Pfeifer (Ed.), Development Human Resources. SanDiego, CA, 1990.

Pasmore,W., *Creating Strategic Change: Designing the Flexible High-Performing Organization,* John Wiley & Sons, New York, 1994, p.p. 50-54.

Peters, T.J. & R.H. Waterman, *In Search of Excellence,* Harper and Row, New York, 1982.

Philips Electronics. *Customer Surveys,* Corporate Quality Bureau, Eindhoven, 1994.

Porter, M.E., *Competitive Advantage,* The Free Press, New York, 1985.

Prins S.J., *Search, report, compare & improve: An orientation study for the purpose, possibilities and use of benchmarks in the performance measuring system,* Moret Fonds Foundation, Rotterdam, 1997.

Quinn, R.E. et al., *Becoming a Master Manager,* John Wiley & Sons, New York, 1996.

Thomas, A., *Coaching for Staff Development,* The British Psychological Society, Leicester, 1995.

Rampersad H.K., *Integrated and Simultaneous Design for Robotic Assembly,* John Wiley & Sons, New York, 1994.

Rampersad H.K., *A Case Study in the Design of Flexible Assembly Systems,* The International Journal of Flexible Manufacturing Systems, Vol. 7, No. 3, pp. 255-286, Boston, 1995.

Rampersad H.K., *The House of DFA,* Proceedings of the IEEE International Symposium on Assembly and Task Planning, pp. 312-318, Pittsburgh, 1995.

Rampersad H.K., *Robotic Assembly System Design for Total Productivity,* International Journal of Production Research, Vol. 34, No. 1, pp. 71-94, London, 1996.

Rampersad H.K., *Application of Design & Process FMEA in the production of steppers,* ASM Lithography, Veldhoven, 1996.

Rampersad, H.K,. *Strategic management; a visionary approach,* Kluwer Bedrijfsinformatie, Deventer, 1997.

Rampersad, H.K., *Knowledge as a strategic production factor,* Inaugural speech. Anton de Kom University of Suriname, Paramaribo, 1998.

Rampersad H.K., *Total Quality Management; a strategy for continuous improvement,* Kluwer Bedrijfswetenschappen, Deventer, 2000.

Rees, J. & P. Rigby, *Total Quality Control – The Hewlett-Packard Way,* in Chase, R.L. (ed), Total Quality Management, IFS, 1988.

Reik, T., *Listening with the third ear,* Pyramid Publications, New York, 1972.

Remmerswaal, J., *Guiding groups,* Bohn Stafleu Van Loghum, Houten, 1992.

Roozenburg, N.F.M. & J. Eekels, *Product Design, Structures and Methods,* John Wiley & Sons, New York, 1995.

Schein, E., *Organizational Culture,* American Psychologist, February 1990, p. 114

Senge, P.M., *The Fifth Discipline: The Art & Practice of the Learning Organization,* Doubleday, New York, 1990.

Slack, N. et al., *Operations Management,* Pitman Publishing, London, 1995.

Thomassen, J.P., *Customer? Which customer?,* Intermediair, 33e jaargang no. 17, Amsterdam, 1997.

Veld, in 't., *Analysis of organizational problems,* Stenfert Kroese, Leiden, 1988.

Weggeman, M., *Knowledge management: design and control of knowledge intensive organizations,* Scriptum, Schiedam, 1997.

Index

About the author

Hubert Rampersad is an international consultant in the field of Total Quality Management, Strategic Management, Business Process Reengineering, and Engineering Design. He received his education in The Netherlands earning his BSc degree in Mechanical Engineering from Enschede Polytechnic, and his MSc degree in Mechanical Engineering from Delft University of Technology where he specialized in manufacturing processes and assembly automation. He received his PhD degree in Industrial Engineering and Management Science from Eindhoven University of Technology. He has authored four books and sixty articles in the field of Management Development and Engineering Design in international journals and conference proceedings. He was connected to the faculty of Business Administration at the Erasmus University Rotterdam as lecturer in Operations Management, and as lecturer in Production Technology to the faculty of Technology Management at the Technical University Eindhoven (The Netherlands). Presently, he is associated with the Anton de Kom University of Suriname as professor in Operations Management & Production Technology. Currently he is also connected to Exaide (the e-Business Architect), which advises traditional companies to transform e-Business ambition into business as usual. Exaide has offices in the United States and the Netherlands. Professor Rampersad can be contacted by e-mail at: hubert_rampersad@hotmail.com.

Druck: Strauss Offsetdruck, Mörlenbach
Verarbeitung: Schäffer, Grünstadt